The Home Boss Toolkit

Branding Success for Self-Publishers

By Nuria Corbi

Book Cover by Nuria Corbi

1st edition 2023

ISBN 978-1-7394865-0-1

Homeboss Media

Find more information at thehomeboss.com or email info@thehomeboss.com

About the Author

Nuria Corbi is a multifaceted entrepreneur, graphic designer, and self-publishing expert with a passion for empowering others to achieve success in their creative pursuits. Born in Spain and raised in Germany, Nuria has called London home since 1982, where she has cultivated a diverse and accomplished career spanning various industries.

With a diploma in graphic design, a certificate in foreign language teaching, and business studies under her belt, Nuria has an impressive background that has informed her approach to branding and self-publishing. Throughout her entrepreneurial journey, she has owned and operated several businesses, including a bakery shop, a language school, an online jewellery business, and a gardening blog. Since 2019, Nuria has been actively publishing on Amazon KDP, sharing her wealth of knowledge and experience with aspiring self-publishers.

Nuria is also the creator of the popular YouTube channel, The Home Boss, where she shares valuable tips and insights on creating a thriving business from home through self-publishing. As an award-winning children's book author, she has developed a highly sought-after Children's Book Course, teaching others how to write and publish captivating children's picture books. Many of her students have gone on to publish remarkable books that have also won awards.

In "The Home Boss Branding Toolkit: Mastering Branding for Self-Publishers," Nuria combines her expertise in design, business, and self-publishing to provide a comprehensive guide for those looking to elevate their branding game. Drawing from her own successes and challenges, Nuria offers valuable insights and practical advice for authors and creative entrepreneurs alike.

When not immersed in her many ventures, Nuria enjoys life in London with her husband and family, indulging in her love of books, gardening, good food, and coffee. Her passion for life and learning is evident in all she does, making her an inspiring figure for those embarking on their own self-publishing journey.

Connect with Nuria Corbi on social media or visit her website for more resources, tips, and inspiration on mastering the art of branding for self-publishers.

The Home Boss website: https://thehomeboss.com

Contents

Dedication

To my loving husband and wonderful children

This book is dedicated to you, the pillars of strength and inspiration in my life. Your unwavering support and encouragement have been my guiding light, giving me the courage to embark on this incredible journey.

Thank you for believing in me, even when I doubted myself. Your love and laughter have filled my heart and fuelled my passion for writing. May this book be a testament to our shared dreams and the beautiful life we've built together.

With all my love and gratitude.

Chapter One

Brief Introduction

Who am I?

Welcome to the exciting world of self-publishing and branding! My name is Nuria Corbi, and I've been enjoying success in self-publishing on Amazon KDP since 2019. Before embracing the self-publishing adventure, I explored various online and offline businesses, including running a gardening blog, an online jewellery store, a language school in sunny Spain, a cute bakery shop, and a translating and interpreting business.

You may know me from my YouTube channel, "The Home Boss," or my website, "thehomeboss.com," where I'm passionate about helping people generate income online through self-publishing and digital products. I find great joy in showing others how this can positively transform their lives, just like it did for mine.

In this book, I'm thrilled to share my experiences and insights with you. Whether you're just getting your toes wet in self-publishing or you're an old hand, my tips are here to help you reach your publishing goals. I'll be your guide through everything you need to know about creating and promoting a fantastic brand identity for your business.

Sure, branding low-content books has its unique challenges, but the principles for building a rock-solid, instantly recognisable brand are universal and apply to all sorts of books. From crafting low-content books like journals and planners to penning fiction and non-fiction, the same branding rules apply.

Consider this book your all-in-one toolkit for developing a distinctive and successful brand identity, no matter the type of book you publish. You'll master how to nail down and convey your brand's values, your target audience, your unique brand voice, and your visual identity while promoting and protecting its reputation. I'll walk you through techniques and strategies to build a compelling brand that truly resonates with your readers and stands out in the packed book market.

And to keep things fun and relatable, I've woven in fictional examples and case studies to show how these concepts and strategies apply to both low-content and traditional fiction and non-fiction books. This way, you get a clear picture of how to adapt these branding strategies to your specific book type, setting you on the path to self-publishing triumph.

In the bustling world of self-publishing, having a strong and recognisable brand is crucial for standing out and achieving your publishing goals. I'll also guide you through the main building blocks of your brand, such as setting up your author central page on Amazon, developing your website, and leveraging the power of social media.

To maximise the benefits of this book, it's essential to stay focused and committed. I recommend setting aside time to work through the topics and complete the exercises. Taking notes and reviewing the material regularly can also be incredibly helpful for reinforcing your learning.

This book isn't meant to be a dull, technical manual on branding. Instead, I hope it's a useful and fun companion that makes the branding process engaging. I want the information to be digestible and actionable, so you can take joy in building your brand and seeing tangible results. I want you to feel thrilled and assured about creating a brand that genuinely mirrors you and connects with your readers.

So, are you ready to dive in and make your brand the next big thing in self-publishing? I'm eager to start this journey with you and can't wait to celebrate your wins.

Let's do this together!

Chapter Two

What is Branding?

Branding in a Nutshell

Ready to decode the mystery of branding? Let's consider it your secret sauce—a special recipe to make your self-publishing business stand out from the crowd!

Before we take a deep dive, let's get on the same page about what branding actually means. In a nutshell, branding is your business's unique fingerprint. It sets you apart from the competition and tells the world, "Hey, this is who I am."

Branding isn't just about designing a cool logo or picking a catchy name. It's a whole lot more! It's about creating a persona for your business, your core values, the story you want to tell, and the feelings you want to stir up in your readers.

From a consumer's perspective, branding is like getting to know a friend. It's about understanding what a company stands for and how others perceive it. It helps you decide if this is a company you want to stick with. If a company claims to be all about saving the environment but doesn't walk the walk, people's perception of the brand will be unfavourable.

When cooking up your own brand, it's vital to see things from your target market's point of view. Your brand should be like a magnet, pulling in those who share your values and preferences. Try to build a story, image, and reputation that strike a chord with your audience, making them feel instantly connected to your brand. This way, you'll gain their trust and loyalty, encouraging them to choose you over others and, ultimately, growing your readership.

In a nutshell, crafting a killer brand is not just about what you want to say but also about what your readers are looking for. A well-thought-out brand can be your ticket to building trust, gaining credibility, and becoming a reliable choice for your readers. It can streamline the promotion of your books, foster a loyal fan base, and eventually boost your sales.

So, let's buckle up and embark on this journey to create your unique superpower for your self-publishing venture! Are you in?

The Art of Author Branding

Throughout my own journey as an author, I've successfully built multiple brands for my books, which have resonated with readers and increased sales. I wrote this book not only to share my expertise but also to genuinely help you elevate your publishing business. I'm convinced that putting your energy into creating a robust, consistent brand can be the key to unlocking greater success and, yes, supercharging your book sales.

So, why is branding such a big deal for authors and their publishing ventures? Let's put on our explorers' hats and dive deep into the exciting world of self-publishing and unravel the wonders of branding!

Don't be fooled; branding isn't just a fancy buzzword. It's a critical piece of the puzzle for anyone looking to win in the self-publishing arena. It's the magic wand that helps you build a bridge of trust and credibility with your readers. It lets you showcase your core values, the audience you're aiming for, and the unique selling points that set your book apart. And guess what? This all leads to readers choosing your book over others in the expansive book market jungle.

But hold on, there's more! Branding also acts like your spotlight, helping you and your books stand out in the crowd. Picture it as crafting a standout ensemble for your book, with a captivating cover, consistent series branding, and a unique colour palette. A good-looking and easily identifiable brand can turn your book into a reader magnet.

Plus, a solid brand helps create a sense of community amongst your readers, nurturing a loyal fan club that not only repeatedly purchases your books but also can't stop talking about them to others. Branding is also your secret weapon in marketing and promoting your books. With a well-crafted brand, you can design laser-targeted marketing campaigns that hit the sweet spot with your audience, successfully highlight your book's worth, and reach potential readers with a strong online presence and savvy social media tactics.

I'm sharing what worked for me in the hope that it will fire you up and equip you to take your author brand to the next level.

By sharing the experiences and strategies that worked for me, I hope to inspire and empower you to elevate your own author brand. Think of branding as the ultimate accessory for your self-publishing journey, allowing you to build trust, establish a unique identity, grow a loyal fan base, and efficiently promote your book. Never underestimate the power of branding—it could be the game-changer that transforms your self-publishing endeavour from a flop to a resounding success story!

Author Brand or Publishing Brand?

When you start your self-publishing journey, it's important to know the difference between an author brand and a publishing brand. Each one offers a unique way to share your work with readers.

An author brand is all about you, the writer. It includes your writing style, your values, and what makes you special compared to other authors. It's like your personal touch on the books you write.

A publishing brand, on the other hand, is about the publisher and the books they create. It covers things like the kinds of books they make, their values, who they want to reach, and the image they want to project. A publishing brand can work with many authors, and each author can have their own author brand.

To decide which one is the best fit for you, consider your goals and your vision. Here are some points to ponder:

- Are you a newbie author looking to carve out your name in the writing world? An author brand might be your best bet.

- Do you see yourself as part of a larger publishing consortium, or perhaps you have a soft spot for the business side of publishing? A publishing brand could be a snug fit for you.

- Reflect on the audience you're aiming to reach and the image you wish to project. An author brand tends to be more niche-focused, while a publishing brand could encompass a wide range of books.

- Consider your long-term plans. If you want to grow into a big publishing company, a publishing brand might be better. But if you just want to focus on writing and your personal image, an author brand could be the way to go.

In my own experience, I've developed both an author brand and a publishing brand. My author brand is focused on a single pen name and is recognised for a specific style and niche of books. I consistently create books in this niche, maintaining a signature style that readers can easily identify. On the other hand, my publishing brand encompasses multiple author names and a variety of book types across different niches. The common thread linking these diverse books is a shared target audience, making it easier to cater to their interests and preferences.

Let's take a look at a fictional example for each type of brand.

Author Brand Example: Meet Emma Wordsmith, a mystery author known for her captivating, atmospheric novels set in quaint English villages. Emma has developed a loyal fan base that eagerly awaits each new book release, knowing they can expect a gripping mystery wrapped in an enchanting setting. Emma's author brand is focused on her unique storytelling abilities, and she maintains a consistent style and niche throughout her works.

Publishing Brand Example: Imagine a publishing house called "Lush Worlds Publishing," which brings together a collection of authors writing in different genres such as romance, fantasy, and science fiction. The common element among these diverse authors and genres is their focus on immersive world-building, creating vivid and imaginative settings for their stories. The publishing brand unites these authors under a shared target audience, catering to readers who seek books with intricate, well-developed worlds.

Let's also check out a couple of fictional branding examples for low-content books.

Author-Brand Example – Jane Doe's Serenity Journals: Jane is known for crafting guided journals and planners designed to nurture well-being and self-care. Her brand, Serenity Journals, offers stunning, thoughtful, and inspiring low-content books that guide readers towards peace, equilibrium, and personal growth. The brand carries a soothing colour palette, elegant fonts, and nature-inspired illustrations. Jane's audience? Individuals seeking tools for self-reflection, relaxation, and personal betterment.

Publishing Brand Example – Vibrant Life Press: This publishing brand churns out a broad array of low-content books, ranging from journals and planners to activity books. The brand's mission is to offer a rich selection of high-quality, visually pleasing, and engaging books catering to diverse interests. Despite being home to different authors, all the books under Vibrant Life Press share a common goal of encouraging a lively, satisfying, and balanced life. The publishing brand is celebrated for its bold colours, dynamic designs, and ingenious concepts that resonate with a broad audience seeking tools for organisation, self-improvement, and leisure pursuits.

Whether you lean towards an author brand or a publishing brand, remember that the choice is yours and should reflect your unique dreams and aspirations. Savour the creative process and let your love for storytelling steer your path. After all, branding is all about building a bond with your target audience and amplifying your distinctive voice in this grand orchestra of words.

"The most valuable asset in any business is the trust and loyalty of its customers."

Chapter Three

Your Mission Statement

A Guide To Purposeful Statements

What is a mission statement, and why should you have one?

You may have heard the term 'mission statement'. What exactly is it? It's all about creating a clear and concise message that sets you apart from the competition and clearly communicates your brand's purpose, values, and goals.

Think of a mission statement as your brand's superpower. It gives you the ability to fly high above the competition and shine bright like a beacon, leading your readers to your books. It's like a roadmap for your brand, guiding you to always make decisions that are in line with your vision and values.

Creating a mission statement is like writing the script for your brand's story. It helps you focus on what truly matters and what you want to achieve. It's a way to communicate your brand's values, vision, and goals to your readers, employees, and partners, creating a sense of direction and purpose for your brand.

You could also think of it as a blueprint for your business. It outlines the purpose, goals, and values that guide all decisions and actions for your business. It provides a clear direction and helps to ensure that everything you do is aligned with your overall vision. Just like a blueprint outlines the design and structure of a building, a mission statement outlines the design and structure of your brand, serving as a guide for your business's future growth and success.

And the best part is that it doesn't have to be long or complicated. In fact, it should be short, sweet, and memorable, like a catchy jingle that sticks in your head all day long. It's a good idea to keep it handy and refer to it whenever you're making important decisions or taking actions for your business.

So don't be afraid to spend some time reflecting on what your brand stands for and what you want to achieve. A mission statement is a powerful tool that can help take your brand to new heights.

How would you use your mission statement?

A mission statement is like a map that guides you on your journey to success. It's like a little helper that reminds you of why you started and where you want to go.

You can use your mission statement in various ways. Here are some examples:

1. Decision-making: whenever you are faced with a decision, you can ask yourself, "Does this align with my mission statement?" If it doesn't, it might be a red flag that you should reconsider your action.

2. Branding: your mission statement should align with your overall brand image and messaging. It can guide your branding efforts and help you stay true to your values.

3. Teamwork: share your mission statement with your team (you may have employees or freelancers), creating a sense of unity and purpose and directing everyone's energy towards a shared goal.

4. Marketing: build your marketing message around your mission statement to attract and engage your target audience. Show them what makes your book special and worth choosing over others.

Remember, your mission statement is like a flexible plan for your business, showing the goals, values, and guiding ideas that shape every decision and action. It serves as a foundation for your brand, leading to its future growth and success.

In short, your mission statement is like a loyal friend, making sure you stay focused and on track throughout your self-publishing journey. It's a fun, engaging, and helpful way to ensure you're always moving in the right direction!

"Your mission statement is the heartbeat of your brand, pumping life and energy into every action, every decision, and every connection."

Crafting Your Mission Statement

Let's create your mission statement!

This is one of the most important steps in creating a strong and recognisable brand, so let's dive in!

First things first, let's define again what a mission statement is: a mission statement is a short and sweet statement that defines your business's purpose, goals, and values. It's a quick and easy way for people to understand what you're all about and what you stand for. Think of it like an "elevator pitch" or "60 second pitch" for your brand. It should be concise, clear, and memorable.

Now, let's talk about the process of writing a mission statement. The first step is to identify your business's purpose. Why do you exist? What problems do you solve for your customers? This is the foundation of your mission statement.

Next, think about your goals. What do you want to achieve with your business? What are your long-term and short-term goals? This will help you create a mission statement that is focused and actionable.

Finally, consider your values. What are the guiding principles that drive your business? What do you stand for? This will help you create a mission statement that is authentic and true to your brand.

Once you have identified your **purpose, goals, and values**, it's time to put them all together. Keep it simple, clear, and concise. Avoid using jargon or buzzwords, and make sure your mission statement is easy to understand.

Here are a few **examples of mission statements** to help you get an idea of how they're crafted:

- "Our mission is to provide affordable and high-quality journals and planners that help people stay organised and achieve their goals."

- "Our mission is to create fiction and non-fiction books that entertain, educate, and inspire readers."

Keep in mind that a mission statement is not a "set it and forget it" kind of thing. It's a living document that should evolve and adapt as your business grows. So don't be afraid to revisit and update your mission statement as needed.

Writing a mission statement can seem hard, but if you follow these steps and keep in mind your purpose, values, and target audience, you can make a mission statement that truly represents your brand and helps you attract your ideal customers. Remember to keep it simple and easy to understand, and don't be afraid to revisit it and make adjustments as your business grows and evolves.

Here are several **fun and practical exercises** you can use to come up with a mission statement for your publishing brand:

- Word association: write down a list of words that come to mind when thinking about your brand. Then, use those words to write a statement that sums up your purpose, goals, and values.

- Brand personality: think of your brand as a person, and write a statement that captures their personality and what they stand for. For example, "Our mission is to bring a touch of fun and creativity to the world of self-publishing."

- Brand mantra: create a short, catchy phrase that represents your brand's mission. For example, "empowering authors to make an income online." (This is one that I have personally used).

- Brand Story: write a short story or a scenario that captures the essence of your brand's mission. For example, "Our mission is to create captivating stories that resonate with fans who treasure imaginative tales and vivid characters."

Remember, the key is to have fun and get creative with these exercises. The most important thing is to come up with a mission statement that truly represents your brand and what you stand for. And don't worry if it takes a few attempts to get it right. Crafting a mission statement is a process, and it's okay to revise and refine it as you go.

It's also important to keep your target audience in mind when crafting your mission statement. Think about what they need and what problem your brand is solving for them. And make sure your statement is clear, concise, and easy to understand.

Once you have your mission statement, use it as a guide for all your branding decisions. It should inform everything from your book titles to cover designs, marketing strategies, and even the language you use on your website and social media. And make sure it is visible and communicated everywhere.

"A mission statement is the compass of your brand, guiding you towards the summit of your dreams, one purposeful step at a time."

Once Upon A Mission Statement

A Tale Of A Fictional Case Study

The following is a fictional case study, and although it's not a true story, fictional case studies can be a fun and engaging way to learn. It can make the learning experience more memorable and help you better understand the concepts and ideas being presented. And... who doesn't love a good story? So let's dive into this case study:

Meet Sarah; she's an awesome self-published author of children's books. But she was feeling a little down because her books weren't getting the recognition and sales she wanted. She realised that her brand didn't have a clear identity and that her books were getting lost in the sea of other children's books.

But Sarah wasn't one to give up easily; she decided to take a step back and create a super cool mission statement for her brand. To get started, she wrote down a list of words that came to mind when thinking about her brand, like "whimsical", "educational", "inspiring", and "diverse". Then she used those words to craft a statement that embodied her purpose, goals, and values: "Our mission is to empower children of all backgrounds to learn, grow, and dream through whimsical and diverse stories."

With her mission statement set, Sarah was able to make better decisions on her book titles, cover designs, and marketing strategies. She also used her mission statement as a guide for the language she used on her website and social media.

For example, Sarah's mission statement helped her create a more diverse set of characters in her stories, which attracted a more diverse audience. This helped her stand out in the crowded market and increase her sales.

Sarah also found that having a mission statement helped her stay focused and motivated. Whenever she faced a tough decision or felt stuck, she would refer back to her mission statement and ask herself if it aligned with her goals and values.

Thanks to her mission statement, Sarah's brand became more successful and recognisable, and she was able to connect with her readers on a deeper level. It was a fun and practical exercise that helped her take her brand to the next level.

So, if you're feeling a little down about your publishing brand, take a step back and create your own cool mission statement. It might just be the thing that helps you stand out in the crowded world of self-publishing.

Examples of mission statements:

Author brand:

- "Our mission is to inspire readers with stories that spark the imagination and leave a lasting impression."

- "Our mission is to create books that challenge the status quo and provide a fresh perspective on the world."

- "Our mission is to connect readers with characters they can relate to and stories that resonate with their experiences."

- "Our mission is to provide readers with an escape from reality and take them on an adventure they'll never forget."

- "Our mission is to entertain, educate, and inspire readers of all ages with stories that capture the heart and imagination."

Publishing brand:

- "Our mission is to publish diverse and thought-provoking books that challenge the norm and promote social change."

- "Our mission is to be the go-to publishing house for emerging voices and innovative storytelling."

- "Our mission is to create a safe and inclusive space for authors to share their unique perspectives and stories with the world."

- "Our mission is to empower readers to make informed decisions and take action on issues that matter through our books."

- "Our mission is to curate a collection of books that educate, inspire, and entertain readers of all backgrounds."

Low-content book brand:

- "Our mission is to help people stay organised and productive with fun and practical planners."

- "Our mission is to provide creative and affordable solutions for self-expression and self-improvement."

- "Our mission is to empower people to unleash their creativity and potential with our unique journals."

- "Our mission is to make planning and goal-setting enjoyable and accessible with our colourful, engaging planners and journals."

- "Our mission is to help people relax and unwind while unleashing their creativity with our stress-reducing, fun colouring books."

So what have we learned about mission statements?

They're super useful for any type of brand, whether you're an author, a publishing company, or a low-content book creator. A mission statement is like a little roadmap that helps you stay on track and focused on your goals and values. It's a clear and concise message that sets you apart from your competitors and helps you connect with your target audience. By taking the time to craft a mission statement that truly represents your brand's identity, you can make a big impact on the world. Remember to keep it short and catchy, so you can easily remember it and use it as a guide whenever you need it. Let your mission statement be your superpower and help you achieve all your goals!

"A mission statement sets the stage for your brand's story—let it inspire, empower, and guide you towards a successful future."

It's Only A Notebook

Brand Success For Notebook Creators

Could someone who makes simple notebooks create a brand?

Of course they could! In fact, creating a brand for a simple notebook company can be a lot of fun, and it's not as daunting as it might seem at first glance.

When it comes to branding, it's all about the message you want to share and the emotions you hope to spark in your customers. The key here is to let your unique notebook-making style shine!

For example, if you're all about using recycled paper and supporting sustainable living, why not build a brand around those eco-friendly values? You could choose earthy colours, a leafy logo, and a catchy slogan like "jotting down notes for a greener future." Show your dedication to the environment by teaming up with tree-planting organisations or using eco-friendly packaging.

Or maybe you're into self-care and mental health. Then create a brand that speaks to that message. Opt for soft pastel colours, a soothing logo, and a memorable tagline like "taking care of yourself, one page at a time." You could even offer resources or collaborate with mental health experts to provide extra support for your customers' well-being.

Here are some more examples:

1. Minimalist elegance: if your notebook designs embody simplicity and elegance, consider building a brand that reflects these qualities. Use clean, modern typography and a sleek logo to convey a sense of sophistication. Your tagline could be something like "Where simplicity meets style," emphasising the sleek and minimalist nature of your notebooks.

2. Creative expressions: if your notebooks are designed to inspire creativity and artistic expression, craft a brand that celebrates imagination. Use vibrant colours, playful illustrations, and a catchy slogan like "Unleash your inner artist on every page." Consider partnering with local artists or hosting contests to engage your customers and showcase their creativity.

3. Wanderlust journals: if your notebooks are perfect companions for travellers and explorers, create a brand that captures the spirit of adventure. Incorporate travel-themed elements like maps, compasses, or iconic landmarks into your branding. Your tagline could be something like, "Write your journey, one destination at a time." Share travel tips, stories, and itineraries on your blog or social media to inspire and connect with fellow wanderers.

4. Inspirational empowerment: if your notebooks aim to uplift and motivate, build a brand that empowers your customers. Choose bold, uplifting colours, and include inspirational quotes or affirmations on your notebook covers. Your tagline could be something like "Unleash your potential, one page at a time." Share inspirational stories and quotes on social media to create a community of positivity and personal growth.

Remember, the key to creating a brand for a simple notebook company is to infuse it with your unique style, values, and the emotions you want to evoke in your customers. Let your passion and creativity guide you, and don't be afraid to think outside the box. Your brand should authentically represent your products and resonate with your target audience.

There's no limit to the possibilities, and the more unique and personal your brand is, the better chance it has of standing out and connecting with your ideal audience. As you build your brand, don't forget to make use of social media and content marketing to share your story and engage with your customers.

"The power of a notebook lies not in its pages but in the ideas it helps bring to life."

Chapter Four

Mindset is Everything

Unlocking Your Branding Mindset

I learned not too long ago that succeeding in business is all about having the right mindset. Preparing yourself mentally before you create your brand is not just a good idea; I really think it's essential.

Creating a brand can be a fun and exciting process, but it can also be a bit overwhelming at times. Before diving into the nitty-gritty details of branding, it's important to take a step back and prepare yourself mentally.

Here are a few tips for getting into the right mindset before creating your brand:

- Take a deep breath and relax. Branding can be a lot to think about but try not to stress too much. Remember that it's a process, and you can always make changes and adjustments as you go.

- Get inspired. Take a look at other brands in your industry and see what you like and dislike about them. Use that inspiration to come up with ideas for your own brand.

- Define your values and goals. What do you want your brand to stand for? What do you want to achieve with your brand? Having a clear understanding of your values and goals will make it easier to create a brand that aligns with them.

- Be open-minded. Be open to new ideas, and don't be afraid to think outside the box. You never know what great ideas might come from unexpected places.

- And most importantly, have fun! Creating a brand is an exciting opportunity to express yourself and your business, so enjoy the process!

By preparing yourself mentally before diving into the branding process, you'll be more focused, creative, and ready to create a brand that truly represents you and your business.

So, take a deep breath, get inspired, and let the branding magic happen!

It's time to get mentally prepared for building your brand, my friend! A big part of that is having a positive attitude and confidence in yourself as a business owner.

First up, let's talk about staying positive. You know how it's easy to get bogged down by the negatives and stress of running a business? Well, positive thinking helps you shift your focus to the good stuff and all the opportunities out there. It'll keep you motivated, help you overcome obstacles, and help you make better decisions for your business. Plus, it'll attract good energy and opportunities to your brand.

Next, let's talk about having confidence in yourself. This means believing in your skills and abilities and trusting that you can make the right choices for your business. When you have confidence, you'll be able to take risks and make bold moves, communicate your brand's message effectively, and earn the respect of your customers and employees. It's natural to experience moments of self-doubt during the branding process. Confront those doubts head-on and replace them with self-belief. Remind yourself of your accomplishments, talents, and the unique stories you have to share. Surround yourself with a supportive network of fellow authors or mentors who can uplift and encourage you. Trust in your ability to create an impactful brand.

It's also important to stay true to yourself. Authenticity is the cornerstone of a successful brand. Be true to yourself and your values as you build your author brand. Authenticity builds trust and forms a genuine connection with your readers. Don't be afraid to showcase your quirks, share personal stories, or express your opinions. Let your brand reflect who you are as an author and as a person. Remember, there is no one quite like you. Embrace your unique voice, style, and perspective as an author. Celebrate your individuality and let it shine through your brand. Recognise that your distinctiveness is what sets you apart from the crowd and attracts readers who resonate with your work. Believe in your own value and the unique contributions you bring to the literary world.

I'm a big believer in staying consistent and persistent. Building a brand takes time and dedication. Stay committed to the process and remain consistent in your branding efforts. Consistency builds recognition and trust. Keep showing up, even when faced with challenges or setbacks. Celebrate small wins along the way and remember that each step forward brings you closer to your branding goals. And you don't have to do it on your own. Embrace collaboration and foster a sense of community. Connect with fellow authors, readers, and industry professionals. Seek opportunities for partnerships, joint promotions, or guest blogging. Engage with your audience through social media, book clubs, or author events. Building a strong network and engaging with your community will amplify your brand's reach and impact.

Building your brand is an ongoing journey. Embrace a growth mindset that encourages continuous learning and improvement. Be open to new ideas, trends, and techniques in branding. Seek out opportunities to expand your knowledge and skillset. Remember, the more you grow, the stronger your brand becomes.

And don't forget to take care of yourself! Running a business can be stressful, but make sure to take time to rest, eat well, and do things you enjoy. When you take care of yourself, you'll be able to tackle challenges with a clear mind and a positive attitude. So don't underestimate the power of a positive mindset and confidence in yourself as you build your brand. It'll make all the difference!

"Speak to yourself with the same kindness and love you'd offer to someone you deeply care about."

Once Upon a Brand Mindset

A Tale of A Fictional Case Study

For your enjoyment, I present to you yet another fictitious case study. This made-up story can be an entertaining and memorable approach to learning new concepts, similar to my earlier case study about creating a mission statement.

So, let's jump right in and see what this case study has in store for us!

Case study

Let's talk about Jane Smith, a self-published author who is ready to level up her game. She's decided to rebrand her business to reach more readers and sell more books.

Before diving into the branding process, Jane took a step back and asked herself some important questions like, "Why do I write?" and "What do I want to achieve with my business?" She realised that her ultimate goal was to inspire and empower women through her writing.

With this clarity, Jane was able to figure out what made her different, such as writing from a feminist point of view and writing about themes like empowerment and self-discovery. She knew this would make her stand out in the market and attract her ideal audience.

Jane also did her research and got to know her target audience, the women who are looking for uplifting and empowering stories. With this knowledge, she created a brand that spoke directly to them and addressed their needs.

Jane also had a growth mindset, constantly looking for new opportunities to promote her books and connect with her readers. And most importantly, she had confidence in her brand and her abilities as an author. This helped her establish trust and credibility with her readers, resulting in an increase in sales and a wider reach.

In addition to having the right mindset before branding her business, Jane also maintained a positive mindset throughout the entire process. She always looked on the bright side and kept a positive attitude, even when things got tough. This helped her stay motivated, overcome obstacles, and make better decisions.

Having a positive mindset also helped her attract positive energy and opportunities to her business. She was able to see opportunities where others saw obstacles, and she approached challenges with a can-do attitude.

Jane's positive mindset was a key factor in her success. It helped her stay motivated, overcome obstacles, make better decisions, and attract positive energy and opportunities to her business. Her positive attitude also helped her establish trust and credibility with her readers, which in turn helped her increase sales and reach a wider audience.

In short, Jane is the perfect example of how having the right mindset before branding can take your business to the next level. By understanding her purpose, identifying her unique selling points, understanding her target audience, having a growth mindset, and having confidence in her brand, she was able to create a brand that resonated with her target audience and helped her increase her sales and reach a wider audience. So don't underestimate the power of a positive mindset when it comes to branding!

"Give your all and enjoy every step of the journey, because success blossoms when you're passionate about your work. It's up to you to make that choice."

Chapter Five

Goal Setting

Set smart goals to help you!

Goal setting is a great idea when deciding to brand your publishing business because it helps keep you focused and motivated throughout the branding process. Having clear and specific goals can help you create a brand that aligns with your values, goals, and target audience. It also helps you measure the success of your branding efforts and make any necessary adjustments along the way.

When setting goals for your publishing brand, it's important to make them **SMART**. SMART goals are **S**pecific, **M**easurable, **A**chievable, **R**elevant, and **T**ime-bound. This means that your goals should be specific and clearly defined, measurable so you can track your progress, achievable so you can accomplish them, relevant to your business, and have a specific time frame for when you want to achieve them.

SMART goals are a super helpful way to make your objectives clear and easy to achieve. Don't worry; I'll break it down for you in simple terms. SMART stands for:

1. Specific: make your goal precise and clear. Instead of saying, "I want to save money," say, "I want to save $1,000."

2. Measurable: make sure you can track your progress. For example, if your goal is to save $1,000, you can measure your progress by checking your savings account balance each month.

3. Achievable: set a goal that's realistic and doable, considering your current situation and resources. If you've never saved money before, aiming to save $1,000,000 in a year might not be achievable.

4. Relevant: your goal should align with your overall life or career objectives. If you're trying to save money for a vacation, make sure that's a priority and not something you'll regret later.

5. Time-bound: set a deadline or timeframe for reaching your goal. This creates a sense of urgency and helps you stay focused. For example, "I want to save $1,000 in 6 months."

For example, a SMART goal for your publishing brand might be: "To write and publish my next best-selling novel within the next year by completing a detailed outlining and research process, beta-reading with a minimum of 5 readers, and hiring a professional editor."

This goal is **Specific** (writing and publishing a best-selling novel), **Measurable** (completing a detailed outlining and research process, beta-reading with a minimum of 5 readers, and hiring a professional editor), **Achievable** (by utilizing specific steps and resources), **Relevant** (to the author's career and success), and **Time-bound** (within the next year).

Here's an example of a SMART goal for a low-content book creator: "To increase my monthly revenue from low-content book sales by 20% within the next 12 months by diversifying my product line and expanding my marketing efforts on Instagram." This goal is specific (increase monthly revenue by 20%), measurable (by tracking sales and revenue), achievable (by diversifying product lines and expanding marketing efforts), relevant (by focusing on low-content book sales and using Instagram as a marketing platform), and time-bound (within the next 12 months).

Goal setting is a great idea when deciding to brand your publishing business because it helps keep you focused and motivated throughout the branding process. By setting clear and specific goals, you'll be able to create a brand that aligns with your values, goals, and target audience, measure the success of your branding efforts, and make any necessary adjustments along the way. Additionally, setting SMART goals allows you to break down the branding process into smaller, manageable tasks, making it easier for you to focus on one thing at a time. This can help you avoid feeling overwhelmed and increase your chances of success. It is also important to make sure that you set both short-term and long-term goals. Short-term goals can help you stay motivated and make progress quickly, while long-term goals can help you maintain focus and stay committed to the overall vision of your brand.

It is also important to be accountable for your goals. This means setting up a system for tracking progress, reviewing progress, and taking action to stay on track. It is also important to have someone to share your goals with—someone who can hold you accountable and provide you with the necessary support and guidance.

Remember that setting goals is an ongoing process, and it's important to review and adjust them as needed. Your business and the market will change, so it's important to stay flexible and open to adjusting your goals accordingly. With the right mindset, clear and specific goals, and a plan of action, you can be well on your way to creating a strong and successful brand for your publishing business.

Here is an exercise that can help you set SMART goals for your publishing brand:

Start by brainstorming a list of goals for your writing and publishing business. These can be big-picture goals, such as increasing book sales or reaching a wider audience, or more specific goals, such as writing a certain number of books per year or launching a book launch campaign.

Next, take each goal and turn it into a SMART goal by making sure it meets the following criteria:

- Specific: make sure the goal is clearly defined and easy to understand.

- Measurable: make sure the goal is quantifiable and you can track your progress towards it.

- Achievable: make sure the goal is realistic and within your reach.

- Relevant: make sure the goal is aligned with your overall business and writing goals.

- Time-bound: make sure the goal has a specific deadline.

Here are a few examples of how you can turn your goals into SMART goals:

- "I want to increase book sales" becomes "I want to increase book sales by 30% within the next 6 months by rebranding my business and targeting a specific audience."

- "I want to reach a wider audience" becomes "I want to reach a wider audience by launching a book launch campaign on social media and running ads targeting a specific audience within the next 3 months."

- "I want to write a certain number of books per year" becomes "I want to write and publish 2 books per year by creating a writing schedule and setting specific deadlines for each book within the next 12 months."

Once you have your SMART goals in place, create a plan of action and set out the steps you need to take to achieve them. It's also helpful to set up a system to track your progress and make adjustments to your plan as needed.

Lastly, don't be afraid to adjust your goals or create new ones as your business evolves. Remember, the goal is not to be perfect but to make progress, and SMART goals will help you do that.

By following this exercise, you'll be able to set SMART goals for your publishing brand that are specific, measurable, achievable, relevant, and time-bound, which will help you stay focused and motivated throughout the branding process. Remember that setting goals is an ongoing process, and it's important to review and adjust them as needed.

"When you set SMART goals, you're not just chasing dreams, you're crafting a roadmap to achievement."

Chapter Six

Your Target Audience

Tracking Down Your Perfect Brand Admirers

Defining your target audience

Any publishing business, even ones that focus on low-content books, needs to know who their target audience is. Your target audience is the specific group of people who are most likely to buy your books, and understanding who they are and what they want is essential for creating a successful brand.

One of the first things to consider when defining your target audience is demographics. Demographics include characteristics such as age, gender, income, education, and location. These characteristics can provide insight into the types of books and products your target audience is most likely to buy. For example, if you're publishing low-content books such as journals, your target audience may be more likely to be women between the ages of 25 and 45 with a higher education.

Another important factor to consider is psychographics. Psychographics refers to a person's values, beliefs, and interests. Understanding the psychographics of your target audience can help you create a brand that appeals to their values and interests. For example, if your target audience values self-improvement and creativity, you may want to focus on creating low-content books that align with these values, such as goal-setting journals or art journals.

In addition to demographics and psychographics, it's also important to consider what types of problems your target audience is facing. Understanding the pain points of your target audience can help you create products that provide solutions to these problems. For example, if your target audience is busy parents, you may create a low-content book that helps them keep track of their child's schedule or appointments.

Once you've defined your target audience, it's important to segment it. Segmentation is the process of dividing your target audience into smaller groups with similar characteristics. This can help you create more targeted marketing campaigns and products that will appeal to specific subgroups within your target audience.

Don't be discouraged if it takes time to figure out your target audience; it's a process, and it's better to have a clear picture of who you are targeting than a general idea. Keep gathering information and testing your products; it will only help you improve and reach your target audience better.

Here are some examples of how to use demographics, psychographics, and segmentation to define your target audience as a publishing company:

Demographics: your publishing company specialises in children's books. You do research and find that most parents who purchase children's books are middle-class, educated, and have children under the age of 12. This information helps you focus your marketing efforts on parents who fit this demographic and create books that align with their values and interests.

Psychographics: your publishing company specialises in self-help books. You do research and find that your target audience is highly motivated to improve their lives and is interested in self-development topics such as mindfulness, productivity, and relationships. This information helps you focus on creating books that align with their values and interests and tailor your marketing efforts to appeal to their needs.

Segmentation: your publishing company specialises in low-content books such as journals. You do your research and find that your target audience is divided into two main segments: those who want to improve their mental health and those who want to improve their productivity. You can then create different journals for each segment, with different features and designs tailored to their specific needs and interests, and create different marketing strategies for each segment.

All these examples show that, by understanding your target audience's demographics, psychographics, and pain points, you can create a brand that appeals to their values and interests, create products that provide solutions to their problems, and segment your target audience to create more targeted marketing campaigns. This will help increase sales and build a stronger brand.

"Knowing your target audience is like having a secret ingredient; it's what turns a bland brand into a flavourful masterpiece."

Once Upon A Target Audience

A Tale Of A Fictional Target Audience Discovery

To clarify the previous chapter, here's a fictional case study of a low-content book publishing company identifying their target audience:

Meet "Pretty Planners", a low-content book publishing company that specialises in creating custom journals, planners, and notebooks. The company was started by a group of friends who had a passion for organisation and personal development. Initially, they had no clear target audience in mind, so they decided to conduct market research to identify their target audience.

First, they looked at demographics. They found that their target audience was primarily women between the ages of 25 and 45 with a college degree. They also found that their target audience had a median annual household income of $75,000 or more.

Next, they looked at psychographics. They found that their target audience was highly motivated to improve their lives and interested in topics such as goal setting, time management, and mindfulness. They also found that their target audience valued organisation and simplicity.

Finally, they looked at segmentation. They found that their target audience could be segmented into two main groups: busy professionals who wanted to improve their productivity and stay organised, and stay-at-home mothers who wanted to balance their daily activities, family, and personal development.

With this information, Pretty Planners was able to create a brand that appeals to their target audience's values and interests and create products that provide solutions to their problems. They created different journals and planners for each segment, with different features and designs tailored to their specific needs and interests, and different marketing strategies for each segment.

As a result, Pretty Planners has seen an increase in sales and has built a strong and loyal customer base. They have a strong brand that resonates with their target audience, and they're well on their way to becoming a leading player in the low-content book publishing industry.

This case study, although fictional, illustrates how identifying and understanding your target audience can help create a strong and successful brand. By doing market research and learning about the demographics, psychographics, and pain points of your target audience, you can create a brand that speaks to their values and interests, make products that solve their problems, and make targeted marketing campaigns that will increase sales and make your brand stronger.

"When you speak to your target audience, it's like a heartfelt conversation with an old friend—genuine, meaningful, and impactful."

The Audience Hunt

Where Do I Start?

You're probably wondering how you can find the information you need to determine your target audience. How can you find out their age, location, gender, interests, and other details that you need to know?

There are several ways to determine the demographics of your target audience. Here are a few methods you can consider:

- Conduct surveys: you can create a survey and distribute it to your existing audience or potential readers. The survey can include questions about age, gender, occupation, income, location, and interests.

- Analyse social media insights: if you have a social media presence, you can use the insights provided by the platform to analyse the demographics of your followers. This can give you a general idea of your target audience.

- Use Google Analytics: if you have a website, you can use Google Analytics to gather data about your website visitors, such as age, gender, and location.

- Research industry data: you can research industry reports and data to find information about the demographics of readers in your genre or niche.

But what if you don't have a way to reach your current audience, or if you are a new publisher and don't have a following? How can you find this information?

The easiest option, by far, is to study your competitors.

By analysing the content and messaging of your competitors, you can get an idea of the audience they are targeting.

Here are some things to look for when studying your competition:

- Analyse their social media profiles: look at their social media profiles to see who is engaging with their content. Check out their followers, comments, and shares to get an idea of their audience.

- Look at their website and marketing materials: analyse their website and marketing materials to see who they are targeting. Look at the language and visuals they are using to see what resonates with their audience.

- Check out their customer reviews: look at their customer reviews on sites like Amazon or Goodreads. See who is leaving reviews and what they are saying about the book.

- Attend industry events: find out about industry events and conferences to see who is there and who is engaging with your competition. This can give you an idea of who your competition is targeting.

By studying your competition, you can get a better understanding of the demographics of your target audience and tailor your marketing efforts accordingly.

What is a customer avatar?

Imagine you're throwing a party. But instead of just any party, you're throwing a party for one specific person—your ideal guest. To make sure they have the best time, you'd need to know what kind of music they like, their favourite foods, what kind of humour makes them laugh, or what topics they find most interesting. Essentially, you'd need to know as much about this person as possible to tailor the party to their tastes.

Well, a customer avatar (also known as a buyer persona or ideal customer profile) is like the ideal guest at your party. It's a detailed profile that represents your ideal reader—the person who would absolutely love your books, connect with your author brand, and engage with your content. This profile includes information like their demographics (age, location, etc.), reading preferences, interests, challenges, goals, and even where they hang out online.

Creating a customer avatar has several benefits:

1. **Tailored Content:** knowing your ideal reader's interests and preferences helps you tailor your books and content to their tastes, making your work more appealing to them.

2. **Effective Marketing:** understanding your ideal reader's habits, challenges, and goals allows you to create marketing messages that resonate with them and highlight the value of your work.

3. **Better Engagement:** by understanding where your ideal reader spends time online and their communication preferences, you can engage with them more effectively and build a stronger author-reader relationship.

4. **Improved Products:** by knowing your ideal reader's pain points and desires, you can craft stories and content that address their needs and fulfil their desires.

So, creating a customer avatar is like preparing for the perfect party. It helps you understand your ideal reader so well that you can create books, content, and marketing strategies they'll love. And when your readers feel seen and understood, they're more likely to become loyal fans and recommend your work to others. It's a win-win situation!

Creating your customer avatar

Creating a customer avatar is a lot like becoming a detective, piecing together clues about your ideal reader until you have a full picture. Let's break it down into easy steps:

1. **Gather Information:** the first step is to gather as much information as you can about your potential readers. You can do this by conducting surveys, observing social media interactions, reading reviews of your books or similar ones, and even having direct conversations with your readers if possible. Keep an eye out for recurring themes or comments that might give you insights into their preferences, habits, and needs.

2. **Identify Demographics:** demographics are the basic details about your ideal reader, like their age, location, occupation, or education level. These details can help you understand who your reader is and how they might interact with your books.

3. **Understand Reading Preferences:** this is where you dive into your reader's bookish habits. Do they prefer e-books or physical copies? Are they big fans of a particular genre? How often do they read? Answers to these questions will help you understand what kind of books and content to create.

4. **Determine Interests and Hobbies:** learning about your read-

er's interests and hobbies outside of reading can help you make your books and content more relatable and engaging. Maybe your readers love gardening, or they're big sci-fi movie fans. These insights can add depth to your stories and make your marketing more appealing.

5. **Identify Pain Points and Goals:** your reader's pain points and goals are the challenges they face and the things they aspire to. Maybe they're looking for more diversity in literature or they want to learn about a specific topic. By addressing these pain points and goals in your books, you can make your work more valuable and relevant to your readers.

6. **Understand Media Consumption:** knowing where your readers spend time online and what influencers they follow can guide you where to focus your marketing efforts. Maybe they're avid Instagram users, or they love listening to a certain podcast. Meeting your readers where they already are can boost your visibility and engagement.

7. **Note Communication Preferences:** finally, understanding how your readers prefer to communicate can help you engage with them more effectively. Are they more responsive to emails, or do they prefer interacting on social media? Adapting to their communication style can make your messages more welcome and effective.

The key is to remember that your customer avatar is a living, evolving profile. As you learn more about your readers and as they change, you can and should adjust your avatar accordingly. The goal is to keep your books and marketing as relevant and engaging as possible for your ideal reader. After all, the more you understand your reader, the better you can serve them with your work. Happy investigating!

What could a customer avatar look like?

Let's imagine we're creating a customer avatar for a self-published author who writes cosy mystery novels. We'll call our ideal reader "Cosy Mystery Mandy."

Avatar Name: Cosy Mystery Mandy

Demographics: Mandy is a 45-year-old woman living in a small town in the Midwest. She's a high school English teacher who loves her job and has a comfortable income. She's married with two kids and a lovable golden retriever.

Reading Preferences: Mandy loves anything mystery, but her heart belongs to cosy mysteries with strong, relatable female protagonists. She's an avid reader and goes through about three books per month. She prefers physical books and loves the smell of a new book. She usually buys her books online or from her local independent bookstore.

Interests and Hobbies: Apart from reading, Mandy enjoys gardening, cooking, and watching detective shows on TV. She's also part of a local book club that meets once a month.

Pain Points and Challenges: Mandy sometimes struggles to find cosy mysteries that are both suspenseful and lighthearted. She doesn't like graphic violence or foul language in her books. She wishes she could find more books that offer the perfect balance of intrigue, humour, and relatability.

Goals and Desires: Mandy's dream is to have a vast library of her favourite cosy mystery novels. She also wants to discover new authors in the genre who write suspenseful yet lighthearted stories.

Influencers and media consumption: Mandy follows a few of her favourite authors on Facebook and Instagram. She's also part of several online book clubs and cosy mystery forums. She listens to a couple of book-related podcasts and enjoys watching book reviews on YouTube.

Communication Preferences: Mandy enjoys receiving newsletters via email, especially if they include book recommendations or exclusive content from her favourite authors. She appreciates a friendly and informal communication style that makes her feel like she's chatting with a friend.

And there we have it! Cosy Mystery Mandy is our ideal reader. Knowing these details about Mandy, you can now create books and marketing strategies that cater to her specific preferences and needs. It's like you're creating the perfect cosy mystery experience just for her. And chances are, there are many more readers out there, just like Mandy, waiting to discover your books.

What if your perfect customer avatar is you?

When I first dipped my toes into the world of low-content books, I was essentially crafting books that I personally found enjoyable. Similarly, as I ventured into writing children's books, I found myself reflecting on the stories I used to read to my own children during their younger years. I had a clear vision of the stories I wanted to bring to life. In both of these scenarios, I was essentially my own customer avatar.

As an author, you've likely heard the advice to "write what you know." This wisdom often translates into creating characters and stories that stem from your own experiences, perspectives, and understanding. But have you ever considered that this advice could extend to your readers as well? In essence, could you, the author, be the ideal reader of your own book? Could your customer avatar—the detailed profile of your ideal reader—actually mirror you?

When you're just starting your writing journey, one of the simplest ways to define your customer avatar is to look in the mirror. After all, who knows your preferences better than you do? If you're writing the kind of books you love to read, it makes sense that your ideal reader might share a lot of your characteristics.

Think about it. You know your favourite genres, the book formats you prefer, your buying behaviours, and even your pet peeves when it comes to books. All this information forms a solid starting point for your customer avatar. Let's call this avatar—you, the reader—the "Mirror Avatar."

Creating a mirror avatar has several benefits. Firstly, it gives you a clear understanding of your reader because you're essentially picturing yourself. You understand this reader's likes and dislikes and what they're likely to connect with in a story. Secondly, it feels authentic because you're writing for someone who shares your taste in books. You're not trying to guess what someone else might like; you're catering to a reader just like you.

However, as your writing journey progresses, you'll likely interact with a diverse range of readers. You'll receive feedback, observe reader behaviour, and engage with your audience on various platforms. As you gain these real-world insights, you might start to notice that not all your readers are mirror images of you. Some might prefer ebooks, while you love paperbacks. Others might enjoy a faster-paced story, while you prefer a slow burn. These differences don't mean your mirror avatar was wrong; they simply mean it's time for it to evolve.

Adjusting your customer avatar based on reader feedback is a crucial part of your growth as an author. It shows that you're not only listening to your audience but also willing to adapt to serve them better. As you incorporate these insights, your Mirror Avatar begins to transform into a more refined "Reader Avatar"—a profile that, while it might have started with you, now embodies the diverse preferences and habits of your actual readers.

So I would say your customer avatar can start by mirroring you. It's an excellent first step towards understanding your ideal reader. But remember, the world of readers is beautifully diverse, and part of your journey as an author involves exploring this diversity. Be willing to adjust your avatar as you learn more about your audience. After all, every reader you connect with helps you become a better author, one book at a time.

"Creating your customer avatar is like finding a hidden treasure; once you've unlocked it, your brand's true potential shines bright."

Chapter Seven

Your Brand Identity

Discover Your Brand's Personality

Your **brand identity** is like the personality of your business. It's the way that people perceive your business that makes it unique. It includes things like your logo, colours, font, and messaging. Think of it like how you would dress to meet someone for the first time: the way you look and the way you present yourself is your brand identity; it's the first impression that people have of you.

Your brand identity should align with your target audience and the products or services that you offer. For example, if you're a publishing company that specialises in children's books, your brand identity should be fun, colourful, and playful. On the other hand, if you're a publishing company that specialises in business books, your brand identity should be more professional and have a serious tone.

Having a strong brand identity is important because it helps people remember your business and what it stands for. It can also help to build trust and loyalty with your customers.

In summary, brand identity is the way that people perceive your business, and what makes it unique is the personality of your business. It's important to have a strong brand identity that aligns with your target audience and the products or services that you offer. It will help people remember your business and what it stands for, and it can help build trust and loyalty with your customers.

Your **brand value** is like the special powers of your business. It's the unique benefits or qualities that your business offers to customers. It's the reason customers choose your business over others.

For example, if you're a publishing company that specialises in children's books, your brand value could be that you offer high-quality, engaging, and educational content that parents can trust to entertain and educate their children. Or if you're a publishing company that specialises in business books, your brand value could be that you offer practical and actionable advice that helps entrepreneurs and business owners achieve their goals.

Having a strong brand value is important because it helps customers understand why they should choose your business. It also helps to build trust and loyalty with your customers. When people understand the value of your brand, they'll be more likely to buy your products, recommend you to others, and come back to buy more.

In summary, brand value is like the special powers of your business; it's the unique benefits or qualities that your business offers to customers, and it's the reason why customers choose your business over others. It's important to have a strong brand value that aligns with your target audience and the products or services that you offer. This will help customers understand why they should choose your business, and it can also help build trust and loyalty with your customers.

Brand value and brand identity are closely related, as they both play an important role in creating a strong and successful brand.

Brand identity is the visual and messaging aspects of your brand; it's the way that people perceive your business and what makes it unique. It can include things like your logo, colours, font, and messaging. It's the personality of your business.

On the other hand, brand value is the unique benefits or qualities that your business offers to customers; it's the reason why customers choose your business over others. It's the special power of your business.

A strong brand identity helps customers remember your business and what it stands for; it also helps to build trust and loyalty with your customers.

Both brand identity and brand value work together to create a strong and successful brand. A strong brand identity helps to communicate the brand value effectively to the customers, and a strong brand value makes the brand more desirable to them. A good brand identity and value together can help to differentiate your brand from the competition and make it more attractive to the target audience.

Here are a few **examples** of brand values that a publishing business might have:

- Education: this value would be focused on providing educational books and materials that help children and adults learn new things, whether it's a new language or new knowledge about a particular subject.

- Community: this value would be focused on building a sense of community among readers, authors, and the publishing company through social media and events, fostering an active dialogue, and sharing feedback and ideas.

- Accessibility: this value would be focused on making books accessible to people with a wide range of abilities, such as audiobooks and e-books with the option of large print.

These are just a few examples, but there are many other values that a publishing business could adopt. The key is to find values that fit with the mission of your business and resonate with the people you want to do business with.

As you can see, each value can provide different approaches and points of view on the same product, depending on the audience and target market, so it's important to carefully evaluate the values that best align with your business goals and target audience.

"Your brand identity is the story you tell the world; make it authentic, make it inspiring, and watch your audience grow."

Brand Archetypes

The Many Personalities Of Your Brand

Have you ever wondered how to make people connect with your brand? The secret is to give it personality and a voice that people can relate to. And the best way to do that is by using brand archetypes. Archetypes can offer a deep structure for brand storytelling and help forge stronger emotional connections with audiences.

Brand archetypes represent universally understood symbols, characters, or experiences, making them immediately recognisable and relatable to customers. By aligning your brand with a particular archetype, you can create a clear, consistent, and compelling brand identity that resonates with your target audience.

So, what exactly is a brand archetype? It's a set of patterns and characteristics that define who your brand is and how it's perceived by your audience. By understanding your brand archetype, you can better predict your target audience's behaviour and build a more relatable brand identity.

The Swiss psychiatrist Carl Jung identified 12 different archetypes that can help us categorise our brand's personality.

These are the 12 main brand archetypes that companies can choose from, each with its own unique personality and characteristics. These archetypes include:

1. The Innocent

2. The Explorer

3. The Sage

4. The Hero

5. The Outlaw

6. The Magician

7. The Regular Guy or Girl

8. The Lover

9. The Jester

10. The Carer

11. The Creator

12. The Ruler

Here are some common words and traits associated with each of the 12 brand archetypes: This might help you find your own brand archetype:

1. The innocent: pure, optimistic, honest, simple, sincere, and wholesome.

2. The explorer: adventurous, daring, free-spirited, curious, independent, and ambitious.

3. The sage: wise, intelligent, insightful, analytical, and knowledgeable.

4. The hero: courageous, determined, confident, and inspiring.

5. The outlaw: rebellious, bold, unconventional, individualistic, anti-authority, and radical.

6. The magician: enigmatic, imaginative, charismatic, transformative, visionary, and mysterious.

7. The regular guy or girl: authentic, genuine, honest, friendly, dependable, and down-to-earth.

8. The lover: passionate, sensual, romantic, intimate, committed, and idealistic.

9. The jester: playful, witty, irreverent, humorous, entertaining, and lighthearted.

10. The carer: compassionate, nurturing, empathetic, selfless, supportive, and dedicated.

11. The creator: innovative, artistic, imaginative, original, expressive, and inventive.

12. The ruler: authoritative, decisive, powerful, confident, responsible, and strategic.

Of course, these are just generalisations, and each brand archetype can be interpreted and expressed in a way that fits your brand's values and identity.

By figuring out which archetype fits a brand's personality and values best, a company can create a strong identity that sticks with its target audience.

Can we apply this to our publishing brand?

Yes, applying the 12 brand archetypes to your publishing brand can help you create a unique and interesting brand identity that speaks to your target audience. Here are some examples of how you could apply each archetype to your publishing brand:

1. The innocent: this archetype is all about simplicity, honesty, and purity. To apply this, focus on clean designs and straightforward messaging, and emphasise your brand's genuine intentions. For example, choose a simple, easy-to-read font and use clear, concise language in your book descriptions.

2. The explorer: the explorer is curious, adventurous, and seeks new experiences. To bring this to life, share stories of your personal journey, take readers on exciting adventures, and encourage them to discover new perspectives. Use captivating images and engaging storytelling to draw them in.

3. The sage: if you're a sage, you value wisdom and knowledge. Share your expertise by providing insightful content, offering advice, and using well-researched facts. You can incorporate quotes, statistics, or thought-provoking questions to engage your audience intellectually.

4. The hero: heroes are courageous, determined, and driven to make a difference. Showcase your strength and perseverance through stories of overcoming challenges or tackling tough topics in your books. Use powerful language and bold visuals to inspire and motivate your readers.

5. The outlaw: the outlaw is a rule-breaker, a rebel who challenges the status quo. Embrace your unconventional side by using

unique formats, controversial themes, or pushing the boundaries of your genre. Don't be afraid to stand out and make a statement with your brand.

6. The magician: magicians are all about transformation and making the impossible possible. Use your brand to inspire change and empower your readers through your books. Share stories of personal growth, offer tools for self-improvement, and create a sense of wonder and possibility.

7. The regular guy or gal: this archetype is down-to-earth, relatable, and values authenticity. Connect with your audience by sharing your own experiences, being open about your struggles, and using conversational language. Make your readers feel like they're talking to a friend.

8. The lover: lovers are passionate, romantic, and all about creating deep connections. Use emotive language, beautiful imagery, and heartwarming stories to engage your readers on an emotional level. Focus on building a community where your audience feels valued and understood.

9. The jester: if you're a jester, you love to have fun, entertain, and bring joy to others. Inject humour, playfulness, and lightheartedness into your brand. Use witty language, amusing anecdotes, or colourful illustrations to make your readers smile.

10. The carer: carers are compassionate, nurturing, and focused on helping others. Share stories of support, offer guidance, and create a safe space for your readers to share their own experiences. Be a source of comfort and encouragement in your books and online presence.

11. The ruler: rulers are confident, powerful, and strive for excellence. Establish yourself as a leader in your field by sharing expert advice, setting high standards, and demonstrating success. Use a profes-

sional tone and polished visuals to communicate your authority.

12. The creator: creators are imaginative, innovative, and driven to create something of lasting value. Showcase your creative process, experiment with new ideas, and inspire others to embrace their own creativity. Use vivid descriptions, engaging visuals, and unique storytelling techniques to captivate your readers.

Can we apply the brand archetypes to low-content book publishing companies?

Absolutely! The 12 Brand Archetypes can be applied to low-content book creators for their branding, too. Let's explore how you can apply them and take a look at some book examples. Remember to stay true to your chosen archetype to create a consistent and memorable brand identity.

1. The innocent: focus on creating minimalist, clean, and wholesome low-content books. Example: a gratitude journal with simple prompts and soothing colours.

2. The explorer: design books that inspire adventure and self-discovery. Example: a travel bucket list journal with thought-provoking prompts and inspiring quotes.

3. The sage: share wisdom and knowledge through your low-content books. Example: a productivity planner with expert tips and strategies for time management.

4. The hero: empower your readers with books that encourage personal growth and overcoming challenges. Example: a goal-setting workbook with motivational quotes and actionable steps.

5. The outlaw: create unique and unconventional low-content books that challenge the norm. Example: a quirky colouring book featuring unconventional patterns and bold designs.

6. The magician: design transformative low-content books that help readers achieve their dreams. Example: a vision board workbook with inspiring prompts and visualisation techniques.

7. The regular guy or gal: keep your books relatable, down-to-earth, and easy to use. Example: a budgeting planner with simple layouts and everyday language.

8. The lover: create books that evoke deep emotions and connections. Example: a couples' journal with thoughtful prompts for nurturing relationships.

9. The jester: bring joy and levity to your low-content books. Example: a witty activity book filled with entertaining puzzles and humorous illustrations.

10. The carer: designing nurturing and supportive low-content books. Example: a self-care planner with gentle reminders and uplifting affirmations.

11. The ruler: establish authority in your niche by offering high-quality, low-content books. Example: a premium daily planner with a sleek design and well-organised layouts.

12. The creator: showcase your creativity and innovation through your low-content books. Example: an art journal with unique prompts and inspiring mixed-media techniques.

From innocents to creators, each archetype offers unique opportunities to connect with readers on an emotional level, transforming your low-content books from mere products into meaningful experiences. As you continue on your publishing journey, remember that the magic of brand archetypes lies in their ability to bring your brand to life, build lasting connections, and pave the way for long-term success. And the key to successful branding using archetypes is consistency. Every aspect of your business, from your website design to your social media strategy, should reinforce the qualities of your chosen archetype. Also, bear in mind that your archetype should align not only with your business values and goals but also with the expectations and desires of your target audience.

Can a brand have multiple archetypes?

Yes, a brand can have multiple archetypes. In fact, it's common for brands to exhibit characteristics of multiple archetypes, as they often represent different aspects of a brand's personality and values. However, it's important to have a primary archetype that best reflects your brand's identity and values, as this will help you create a consistent brand message and connect with your target audience. Additionally, incorporating secondary archetypes can add depth and complexity to your brand's identity, making it more interesting and memorable.

Brand archetypes help give your publishing business a unique personality, which can make it easier for you to connect with your readers. The interesting part is that, when you really embrace your chosen archetype, it can also inspire you to create books that perfectly match your brand's "vibe." This makes your books even more special and appealing to your audience. By doing this, you can stand out from the crowd and create a strong bond with your readers, making them more likely to come back for more!

"The magic of brand archetypes lies in their ability to bring your brand to life."

Naming Your Brand

The Perfect Fit

I don't know about you, but I think finding a name for your brand is a bit like finding a name for a baby! Not easy!

The easiest way to choose your brand name would be to use your pen name, right? After all, if your pen name is established and already recognised by your audience, then it makes sense to use it as your brand. However, it is ultimately up to you whether your brand name should be the same as your pen name.

Here are a few things to consider when making this decision:

- Established pen name: if you have an established pen name that is well known and recognised by your audience, you may want to use it as your brand name as well. This can help you build on the recognition and reputation you've already established as an author.

- Alignment with your brand image: consider whether your pen name aligns with the image and message you want to project as an author. If your pen name is associated with a specific genre or style and aligns with your brand, then it may be a good choice to use as your brand name. However, if your pen name is not well known or doesn't align with your brand image, you may want to consider choosing a different brand name. It's important to choose a name that will help you effectively connect with your audience and project the image you want to be associated with.

- Opportunities for rebranding: sometimes rebranding is necessary for authors for various reasons, like a change of genre, a shift in focus, or personal reasons. If your pen name is not working out well or no longer aligns with your brand, you may want to rebrand and choose a new brand name. Ultimately, the decision of whether or not to use your pen name as your brand name will depend on your personal preference and your specific goals and circumstances. You can also use a pen name and brand name at the same time, having a pen name for your written work and a separate brand name for yourself as a person, or how you want to be perceived by the public.

Rebranding is obviously best avoided due to the work involved, but life isn't always orderly and simple! If you truly believe that change is important, the best course of action is to embrace it and move forward with it.

In fact, I recently had a similar experience myself. Even though I had published multiple books under a particular pen name, Amazon denied my attempt to publish a new book under that name because they believed it sounded too much like a brand name. This is because Amazon has become stricter about pen names sounding like brand names.

But I found a solution! I found that buying my own ISBNs and stating my brand name as the imprint worked well. This way, my brand name is still searchable and shows up as the publisher on the Amazon book's sales page. This also allows me to publish under different pen names under that overall brand.

So, you could also think about structuring your brand in a similar way. For example, using a brand name like 'Fanfoundry Press' and publishing under different pen names for different genres or types of books like 'Lizzie Smythe' for planners, 'Brad Simmons' for logbooks, or 'Dora Light' for journals and notebooks.

It's all about being flexible and finding ways to make it work. It takes time and effort, but you'll end up with a brand that is unique, recognisable, and adaptable to the changes in the industry.

When deciding what kind of books to have under one brand name, there are a few key factors to consider:

- Genre: one of the most important factors to consider is the genre of your books. If you write books in the same genre, it can be beneficial to keep them under the same brand name. For example, if you write mystery novels, it might make sense to have all of your books under the same brand name. This can help you establish yourself as an expert in that genre and make it easier for readers to find your books.

- Audience: consider the target audience of your books. If your books are targeted at the same readers, then it might make sense to have them under the same brand name. This can help you build a strong community of readers who are interested in the same types of books.

- Style or tone: if your books have a similar style or tone, it could be beneficial to have them under the same brand name. This can help you build a consistent style, and it will make it easier for readers to recognise your books.

- Cohesiveness: the brand name should be cohesive with the books and the author's image; if the books are vastly different from one another, it may not make sense to have them under the same brand. Rebranding: as you write more books, you may change your focus or your writing style; in this case, it would make sense to rebrand so that the name aligns with your current focus, genre, and target audience.

It's important to note that you don't have to limit yourself to only one pen name; you can use different pen names for different types of books or genres. As long as you make sure to keep the branding consistent across each type or genre and that the names are not too similar to existing trademarked names. Ultimately, the decision about what kind of books to have under one brand name will depend on your personal preferences and the goals you have for your brand.

So how do you go about choosing a brand name?

Choosing a brand name for your author or low-content book publishing business can be both exciting and overwhelming. Your brand name is a crucial part of your business and can have a significant impact on how people perceive your books and your business as a whole. In this chapter, we'll go over some tips to help you choose a brand name that you'll be proud of and that resonates with your target audience.

- Keep it simple. A brand name that is easy to pronounce and spell is more likely to stick in people's minds. Avoid using complex words or puns that may be hard to understand.

- Be memorable: Potential customers are more likely to choose a brand name that is memorable and easy to recall. Consider using a play on words or a clever pun to make your brand name stand out.

- Consider your target audience: Think about the types of books you will be publishing and the audience you will be targeting. Your brand name should be relevant and appealing to your target audience.

- Make it unique: Your brand name should be unique and not easily confused with other brands in the market. Conduct a thorough search of existing brand names to ensure your brand name is not already in use.

- Have fun: Choosing a brand name is an opportunity to be creative and have fun. Don't be afraid to think outside the box and consider unconventional names.

- Once you've chosen your brand name, you might think about registering it as a trademark to prevent others from using it.

Where can you get ideas?

There are many different sources you can use to get ideas for brand names. Here are a few tips and exercises to help you choose a brand name:

- Look at your competitors: research other brands in your industry and see what kinds of brand names they use. This can give you an idea of what types of names are popular in your industry and what types of names to avoid.

- Use a thesaurus: use a thesaurus to come up with synonyms and related words for your products or services. This can help you come up with unique and descriptive names that accurately represent your brand.

- Look for inspiration in everyday life: keep an eye out for words and phrases that catch your attention. They can be found on street signs, billboards, newspapers, conversations, etc. These words and phrases can be used as inspiration for your brand name.

- Use online tools: there are online tools such as name generators, brand name suggestion websites, and domain checkers that can help you come up with names.

Some examples of brand-name exercises:

Create a list of keywords and phrases that represent your brand, such as "innovative," "reliable," or "fun." Then use a thesaurus to come up with synonyms and related words.

Look at your competitors' names and try to identify patterns, such as the use of alliteration, puns, or wordplay. Use this as inspiration to create your own unique name.

Think about the emotional connection you want your brand name to create, and brainstorm a list of words and phrases that evoke those emotions.

Create a list of brand name ideas and ask people in your target audience which ones they like best and why.

By working through these exercises, you'll be able to come up with a list of potential brand names that accurately represent your brand and appeal to your target audience. Choosing the right brand name can help you build a strong and memorable brand that resonates with your target audience and differentiates you from your competitors. Keep in mind that a strong brand name is just one aspect of building a successful brand. It should be consistent with your brand values and mission, and it should also align with your brand positioning and messaging.

And here are some creative suggestions for brand name research:

Make up words

Start experimenting with words that are associated with your brand after consulting a dictionary or thesaurus. To create original and memorable names, try fusing them or using a foreign language.

Look to nature for inspiration

Nature can serve as a fantastic source for brand names. Use the names of plants, animals, or places that are associated with your brand.

Make use of wordplay

Consider wordplay or puns related to your brand when coming up with a name; it may be entertaining and memorable.

Consider your personal history

You might want to incorporate a memorable moment, place, or person into your business name to give it a more personal feel.

Ask your family and friends

With the aid of a new perspective, you may occasionally be able to think of a name that you wouldn't have thought of on your own. If you ask your friends and family for their opinions, you might be surprised at the suggestions they have.

Utilise internet resources

A variety of resources are available online that can assist you in developing a brand name, including name generators, domain checkers, and trademark databases. These resources might help you generate a tonne of ideas and come up with the ideal name for your company. Using the Wu Tang Clan name generator, which was also used by actor, comedian, and musician Donald Glover, I came up with one of my brand names. Glover claims that in order to come up with a rap moniker for himself, he employed the generator, and it came up with the name "Childish Gambino" at random. According to Glover, the name appealed to him since it was "fun" and "obviously ironic." The name was first used for his songs, and subsequently it was adopted as his stage name. Glover's stage name has come to be associated with his artistic sensibility and has assisted him in creating a distinctive brand identity in the entertainment sector. Guess what happened when I tried out this fancy generator? It tossed out a brand name that seemed absolutely off-the-wall. But you know what? It had a certain ring to it that I found really appealing. It was a one-of-a-kind name that was catchy enough to keep bouncing around in people's heads. Plus, it had that fun quirkiness that blended perfectly with my brand's vibe. So, all in all, it was a win! You just never know, often the most memorable brand names are discovered in the most unexpected ways. Life's like that, isn't it?

"A great brand name is a beacon, shining brightly and guiding your audience to the unique world you've created."

Once Upon A Brand Name

A Tale Of Another Fictional Case Study

Here's a fictional case study of an author, "Samantha Smith", and how she found a brand name for her publishing brand:

Samantha Smith is a debut author who has just finished writing her first novel. She wants to establish a brand for herself and her book, but she's having a hard time coming up with a name that's both memorable and reflective of her book's content.

Samantha starts by brainstorming a list of keywords that she feels best describe her book, such as "adventure," "mystery," "family," and "empowerment." She also thinks about what she wants her brand to represent, such as her values and the message she wants to convey.

Next, Samantha starts researching similar books and authors to see what kinds of names they have used. She takes note of names that catch her attention and why they work. She also looks at the websites and social media accounts of these authors to see how they present themselves and their brand.

With this information in mind, Samantha starts to play around with different name options, combining her keywords and looking for names that are both memorable and reflective of her book's content. She also checks to see if the names she's considering are available as a website domain, social media handle, or trademark.

After some time, Samantha finally settles on a brand name, "Mystery Adventures," that she feels best represents her book and her brand values. The name "Mystery Adventures" incorporates the keywords "mystery" and "adventure," which are central themes in her book; it's also catchy and memorable. She also checked and found that the name was available as a website domain, social media handle, and trademark.

Samantha creates a logo, branding materials, and a website using the name "Mystery Adventures" and starts to promote her book using her new brand name. She also starts building a following on social media using the same name, and she finds that her audience is responding well to her brand.

As her book's launch date approaches, Samantha finds that her brand name, "Mystery Adventures," has helped her stand out in a crowded market, and her audience is excited about her book. She's been able to establish a strong online presence and build a community of readers who are interested in her work.

Samantha's approach to finding a brand name for her publishing brand can serve as an example for other authors or small business owners who are looking to establish a brand for themselves. It shows how important it is to consider the keywords that best describe your book and your brand values when choosing a name. It also highlights the importance of researching similar books and authors and checking the availability of the name as a website domain, social media handle, and trademark.

Samantha's case study also demonstrates the power of a strong brand name and how it can help an author stand out in a crowded market and build a community of readers. It shows that a well-chosen brand name can be an important tool in positioning a book for success.

I Made a Mistake...

Another thing to consider is whether your brand name is available as a domain name and social media handle, and if you have the legal right to use it. It's important to check the availability of your potential brand name and to research any existing trademarks or copyrights to avoid any legal issues down the road.

I totally understand the struggles of choosing a brand name, and I want to share a mistake I made with my brand, "The Home Boss." I spent a lot of time deciding on this name, and even though I've created multiple brands, it never gets any easier for me. One thing I didn't do, which I wish I had done, was to check if the name was already taken on social media platforms. I bought the domain name, but when I went to create my Instagram account for "The Home Boss," I found that it was already taken! But don't worry; there are ways to work around it. I ended up calling it @thehomebossblog, which isn't ideal but works. The same thing happened on Pinterest, so I created an account named @thehomebossbiz.

My advice to you is to make sure to check that the name you want is not already taken on social media platforms before you buy your domain name. This will save you from a similar situation, and you'll be able to create social media accounts with the exact name you want for your brand. And if the name you want is already taken, you can always slightly modify it, but it's still worth checking beforehand to avoid any confusion.

When you've narrowed down your list of potential brand names, try testing them out on friends, family, and potential customers. Gather feedback and see how they react to the names. Remember, your brand name is a crucial part of your business, and it's worth taking the time to choose the right one. Be proud of your brand name, and let it reflect the quality and value of your books.

"The power of a brand name lies in its ability to evoke emotions, awaken memories, and inspire loyalty in the hearts of your audience."

Your Brand Voice

The Sound Of Your Brand

A brand voice refers to the unique way a business communicates and expresses itself through its messaging, language, and tone. It's the personality and character that a brand projects to its audience through its communications, whether it's through its website, social media, or advertising.

Think of it like this: just like a person has a unique voice, a brand also has its own unique voice that sets it apart from others. For example, a luxury brand's voice might be sophisticated and elegant, while a more casual brand's voice might be friendly and relatable. A brand voice helps to create a consistent message and personality that resonates with its audience and helps to build trust and credibility.

It's important to note that a brand voice should align with the values of the company and target audience. For example, a company that values sustainability and eco-friendliness should have a brand voice that reflects this and appeals to an environmentally conscious audience.

A brand voice, to sum up, is the unique personality and character that a brand projects to its audience through its communications. It helps to create a consistent message and build trust and credibility with the target audience, and it should align with the values of the company and the target audience.

Examples of brands and their voices:

- Scholastic, a publisher of children's books, uses a fun and playful tone in their social media posts and marketing materials. They often use words like "exciting," "adventure," and "fun" to engage their target audience of young readers.

- Hachette Book Group, a publisher of both fiction and nonfiction books, uses a professional and informative tone in their communications. They often use language that reflects their commitment to publishing high-quality content, such as "exceptional," "authoritative," and "groundbreaking."

- Penguin Random House, a large publisher of fiction and nonfiction books, uses a variety of tones depending on the audience and genre of the book. In their social media posts, they often use a more conversational and approachable tone, while in their marketing materials for business books, they use a more professional and informative tone.

- Hay House, a publisher of self-help and personal growth books, uses a positive and uplifting tone in their communications. They often use words like "inspiring," "transformative," and "empowering" to reflect their focus on helping readers improve their lives.

- Inkwell Press is a company that designs and publishes planners and journals. Their brand voice is "organised, productive, and creative." They use a professional and motivated tone, with a focus on helping their customers improve their productivity and organisation. They appeal to people looking for a high-quality and visually appealing planner.

How to develop your brand voice:

- Know your brand values: understand your brand's mission, values, and unique selling points. This will help you identify the type of language and tone that align with your brand.

- Define your target audience: understand the demographics, psychographics, and interests of your target audience. This will help you determine the type of language and tone that will resonate with them.

- Be consistent: establish guidelines for your brand voice and stick to them. Consistency is key to building a strong and recognisable brand voice.

Everything we learned in previous chapters is now going to help us develop our brand voice.

Tips to develop your brand voice:

- Consider the tone and personality that align with your brand values and target audience. For example, if you are a children's book publisher, you may want to use a fun and playful tone, while if you publish business books, a professional and informative tone may be more appropriate.

- Use language and tone that reflect your brand values. If one of your brand values is sustainability, use language that reflects that value in your messaging.

- Be consistent. Use the same tone and language across all channels, including your website, social media, and email communications.

- Write in the first person if your voice is more direct. Writing in the first person can help create a more personal and authentic brand voice. Instead of saying "our company," try saying "we" or "I."

- Identify your brand personality: think about your brand as if it were a person. What is its personality? Is it formal or casual, serious or playful, traditional or innovative? Identifying your brand's personality will help you create a brand voice that aligns with it.

- Define your target audience: understand the demographics, psychographics, and interests of your target audience. This will help you determine the type of language and tone that will resonate with them.

- Evaluate and adjust: continuously evaluate and adjust your brand voice as your brand evolves and as you learn more about your target audience.

- Use a language style guide: create a language style guide that includes guidelines for grammar, tone, vocabulary, and punctuation. This will help ensure consistency in your brand's voice across all communication channels.

What is a language style guide?

A language style guide is a document that establishes guidelines for the language and tone used in a brand's communication. It can include guidelines for grammar, vocabulary, punctuation, and tone of voice. The purpose of a language style guide is to ensure consistency in a brand's communication and to ensure that the communication aligns with the brand's mission, values, and target audience.

For example, a language style guide for a publishing business that targets young adults might include the following guidelines:

- Use informal and friendly language, but avoid slang and offensive language.

- Use active voice rather than passive voice.

- Use contractions.

- Use an informal, fun, and engaging tone of voice.

A language style guide for a professional consulting firm would be different:

- Use formal and professional language; avoid slang and colloquialisms.

- Use proper grammar and punctuation.

- The use of the passive voice is allowed when necessary.

- Use of a formal and confident tone of voice

An example of a language style guide for a low-content book publishing business may include the following guidelines:

- Use simple, clear, and easy-to-understand language.

- Use the active voice.

- Avoid unnecessary jargon or technical terms.

- Use a fun, creative, and inspiring tone of voice.

- Use specific vocabulary that is appropriate for the target audience.

It's important to note that a language style guide is a living document and should be reviewed and updated regularly to ensure it stays relevant and accurate with a brand's target audience and changing trends and language.

Here is an example of a brand style guide for a crime novel author:

1. **Brand Voice and Tone:**

- Develop a brand voice that is intriguing, engaging, and reflective of your crime fiction writing style.

- Ensure that all promotional materials and online interactions have a consistent tone that aligns with your author persona and the themes of your novels.

2. **Visual Identity:**

- Design a logo that represents your brand, incorporating elements related to crime fiction, such as a magnifying glass, a typewriter, or a mysterious silhouette.

- Choose a colour palette that evokes the atmosphere of your novels, such as dark shades or moody colours, and use it consistently across all branding materials.

- Select fonts that are easy to read and have a professional appearance. Consider using a combination of serif and sans-serif fonts for variety and visual interest.

3. Social Media Presence:

- Maintain a consistent posting schedule on your chosen social media platforms to keep your audience engaged and informed.

- Share content related to your novels, such as teasers, behind-the-scenes insights, and glimpses into your writing process.

- Engage with your audience by responding to comments and messages, as well as sharing content from fellow crime fiction authors and industry influencers.

4. Website and blog:

- Create a visually appealing and user-friendly website that showcases your novels, author bio, and any upcoming events or appearances.

- Include a blog where you can share articles and insights related to crime fiction, the writing process, and the inspiration behind your novels.

- Optimise your website for search engines (SEO) to increase visibility and attract new readers.

5. Email Newsletter:

- Send regular email newsletters to your subscribers, sharing updates about your novels, upcoming events, and any promotions or giveaways.

- Maintain a consistent visual and written style in your newsletters that aligns with your overall brand identity.

- Encourage reader engagement by including exclusive content, such as sneak peeks, author interviews, or book recommendations.

6. Promotional Materials:

- Design eye-catching promotional materials, such as bookmarks, postcards, or posters, that feature your brand's visual identity and showcase your novels.

- Create a consistent and cohesive look across all promotional materials using your chosen colour palette, fonts, and logo.

By following this brand style guide, you'll establish a cohesive and memorable presence for your crime novel author brand, helping you connect with your target audience and grow a loyal reader base.

What if you're finding writing in your brand voice too difficult?

If you are not a confident writer or struggle to find the right words to convey your brand's personality, it may be helpful to consider outsourcing this task to a professional writer or marketing agency. This is why it is so important to know your brand voice so that you can clearly communicate it to the writer.

Here are some helpful points to consider when outsourcing the development of your brand's voice:

- Clearly communicate your brand values and target audience. It's important to provide the writer or agency with a clear understanding of your brand values and target audience. This will help them create a brand voice that aligns with your goals and resonates with your intended audience.

- Look for writing samples: when choosing a writer or agency, look for samples of their work to ensure that their style aligns with your vision for your brand's voice.

- Establish guidelines: establishing guidelines for your brand voice, such as tone, language, and messaging, can help ensure that the final product is consistent with your brand identity.

- Review and collaborate: don't be afraid to ask for revisions or to provide feedback on the writing. Collaborating with the writer or agency will help ensure that the final product accurately reflects your brand's voice.

Outsourcing the development of your brand's voice can be a cost-effective and efficient way to ensure that your brand's personality is well-defined and consistently conveyed to your audience. By following these helpful points and collaborating with a professional writer or agency, you can create a brand voice that truly reflects your values and resonates with your target audience.

Where can you find writers or agencies?

There are many websites and platforms that offer professional writing and branding services, including:

Upwork is a freelance platform that connects businesses with a global network of professional freelancers. You can find writers and marketers with experience in branding and voice development on Upwork.

Fiverr is a platform that allows businesses to find and hire freelancers for a variety of services, including writing and branding. You can find writers and marketers with experience in branding and voice development on Fiverr.

Contently is a content marketing platform that offers a range of services, including brand voice development.

Textbroker is a platform that connects businesses with a network of professional writers. You can find writers with experience in branding and voice development on Textbroker.

These are just a few examples I found at the time of writing this book, and there are many other websites and platforms that offer similar services. It's a good idea to do your research and read reviews before choosing a platform or writer to work with.

"Your brand voice is your reader's first impression of your work"

Your Brand's Visual Identity

The Art Of Perception

When we think about branding, we're usually thinking of the visual aspect – the way a brand looks, the unique aesthetic and impression a brand projects to the world. The vibe and style that a brand shows off to everyone.

Well, this is the brand's visual identity. A visual identity is a super important part of how your brand comes across to people. It's like the face of your brand, and it helps people remember and recognise you. In this chapter, we'll talk about what makes up a visual identity and how you can create one that's perfect for your brand.

Why Visual Identity Matters

Your visual identity is like a big, colourful hug that brings together all the visual parts of your brand. It includes things like your logo, colours, fonts, and images. A great visual identity:

- makes your brand easy to recognise and remember.

- shows off your brand's personality and values.

- makes people feel a certain way about your brand.

- builds trust and credibility.

- helps you stand out from the competition.

The Pieces of a Visual Identity Puzzle

- Logo: your logo is like a little flag that represents your brand. It should be simple, easy to use in different situations, and memorable.

- Colour palette: colours can say a lot about your brand and how they make people feel. Pick colours that match your brand's personality and vibe.

- Typography: the fonts you use are also part of your visual identity. Make sure your fonts look good with your logo and colours, and stay consistent in everything you do.

- Imagery: the pictures, illustrations, and other visuals you use are part of your brand's look, too. Stick to a style that fits your brand and appeals to your target audience.

Let's talk about your logo first

A well-designed logo is the foundation of a company's brand and can help establish credibility, communicate values, and make a lasting impression on readers. Designing a logo might seem like a daunting task, but don't worry; it's not as hard as it seems. By following a few key principles and studying examples of successful logos in the industry, you'll be able to create a logo that truly represents your company and resonates with your audience.

- Simple and memorable: the most successful logos are simple and easy to remember. A complex logo with too many elements can be difficult for people to recall and may not stand out as well. A simple logo with clean lines and a clear message is more likely to be remembered and recognised. For example, the Penguin Random House logo is a simple and memorable design featuring a stylized penguin with the company name.

- Versatile: your logo should be versatile enough to be used in a variety of contexts, such as on book covers, websites, and marketing materials. It should also be able to be reproduced in a variety of sizes and formats without losing its clarity and impact. For example, the Simon & Schuster logo features a simple yet versatile design that can be used across different mediums and formats.

- Meaningful: the logo should convey the company's mission, values, and personality. The design should be reflective of the company's focus and what it stands for. For example, the Oxford University Press logo used to feature an image of the iconic Oxford University Bodleian Library (before they rebranded), which is instantly recognisable and meaningful as a symbol of the company's commitment to education and scholarship.

- Timeless: a logo should be designed to stand the test of time. Avoid trends and fads that may quickly become dated. Choose colours, fonts, and imagery that are timeless and will still be relevant in years to come. For example, the British tea company Twinings has a logo designed in 1787, that has remained unchanged for many years and still maintains its timeless appeal.

- Professional: your logo should look professional and polished. You could try designing it yourself or hire a qualified designer or design company to do it for you who can guarantee the logo's high quality. More on that later.

In conclusion, a well-designed logo is a crucial element in creating a strong brand identity for a publishing company. A logo should be simple and memorable, versatile, meaningful, timeless, and professional. By following these guidelines and studying examples of successful logos in the industry, you can create a logo that effectively represents your company and resonates with your audience.

Could you design a logo yourself?

I have so far designed all the logos for my brands myself, with the help of a design tool called Canva. You may be familiar with this tool, but if not, Canva is a really user-friendly tool that helps you design all kinds of graphics that you can use in your business without any prior design experience. When I was very young, I did train as a graphic designer (back in the days of no computers), and I also gained my work experience for school at a graphic design studio in Germany. But in those days, things were very different. Everything had to be done manually; there were no computers.

I remember using Letraset to add text to graphics. This was a brand of rub-down transfer lettering sheets that allowed designers and illustrators to easily add text to their designs.

The process of using Letraset involved selecting the desired letters or words from a sheet, rubbing the back of the sheet to transfer the lettering onto a surface, and then positioning the letters onto the design. The letters were made of a thin, semi-transparent material that allowed for easy adjustments and repositioning.

Letraset sheets came in a wide variety of typefaces and sizes, making them versatile for different design projects. They were widely used in various fields such as graphic design, advertising, packaging, and even comic book lettering.

At the time, it was a cost-effective and efficient way to add text to designs, as it eliminated the need for hand lettering or typesetting equipment.

How times have changed! With the advent of digital design tools, we now have the ability to easily create and edit text on a computer, and Letraset has largely been replaced by digital methods.

You may wonder if you can still design your own logo without graphic design experience, and to that I would say, give it a try! Canva has a free version if you want to try it out, and it also has templates that you can use to base your design on. Make sure to read their licencing terms to be safe regarding copyright and trademarking your logo and to make sure it's the right option for your business. If you enjoy the creative process, then it could be a good alternative to using a professional designer. But if your budget allows it, outsource this task to a professional who will ensure that the logo is of high quality and meets industry standards.

If you're looking to outsource the logo creation for your brand, there are a few options you can consider. Here are a few tips to help you choose the best one for your needs:

Crowdsourcing platforms: websites such as 99designs, Crowdspring, and DesignCrowd allow you to post a design brief and receive multiple designs from designers all over the world. This can be a great option if you want to see a variety of designs and get feedback from a community of designers.

When outsourcing your logo creation, it's important to have a clear idea of what you want, provide a detailed design brief, and communicate effectively with the designer. It's also a good idea to ask for multiple revisions to ensure that you're satisfied with the final product.

What makes a good logo?

A good logo is an essential component of a strong brand, and it's important to make sure that it is well-designed and reflective of your brand's values and message.

A great logo should be simple and easy to recognise, even when it's reproduced in a small size or in black and white. It should be designed in a way that is consistent with your overall branding strategy, and it should be memorable and timeless. This means that it should be able to stand the test of time and not look outdated in a few years.

It should be designed in such a way that it is consistent with the overall branding strategy. For example, a playful and colourful logo would be more appropriate for a children's brand, while a sleek and modern logo would be more fitting for a technology company.

Additionally, a good logo should be versatile and work well in different contexts, such as on a website, social media, business cards, and advertising materials. It should also be easy to reproduce and look good in both digital and print formats.

Let's talk about your colour palette

Ready to give your brand some colour? Picking the right colours for your brand can really make it shine and connect with your audience. Let's explore how to find the best colour palette that reflects your brand's personality and makes it pop!

Why Colours Matter

Colours can do wonders for your brand. They're like a visual language that helps people understand what your brand is all about. Plus, the right colours can make your brand look amazing and leave a lasting impression. Here's why colours are so important:

- They create a certain mood and atmosphere.

- They express your brand's personality.

- They make your brand easy to recognise.

- They help you stand out from the competition.

- They evoke emotions and influence how people feel about your brand.

Understanding colour psychology

Colours can have a powerful effect on our emotions and how we perceive things. That's why it's super helpful to know a bit about colour psychology when choosing your brand's palette. Here are some common colour associations to keep in mind:

- Red: passion, energy, excitement

- Blue: trust, calmness, and stability.

- Yellow: happiness, optimism, warmth.

- Green: growth, nature, balance.

- Orange: creativity, enthusiasm, playfulness.

- Purple: luxury, spirituality, mystery.

- Black: power, sophistication, elegance.

- White: simplicity, purity, cleanliness.

With this in mind, how can we go about finding our colour palette?

- Define your brand's personality: before you start picking colours, take some time to think about your brand's personality, values, and target audience. This will help you choose colours that feel just right for your brand.

- Look for inspiration: keep your eyes open for colour inspiration everywhere you go! Look at other brands, design trends, and even nature to find colours that speak to you.

- Start with a base colour: pick a main colour that captures the essence of your brand. This will be the foundation of your colour palette, and the other colours you choose should complement it.

- Add supporting colours: choose two or three supporting colours that go well with your base colour. These colours can be used for accents, backgrounds, and other design elements.

- Consider contrast and harmony: make sure your colours work well together and create a nice balance. You want your palette to be visually appealing but also easy to read and understand.

- Test your palette: try out your colour palette on different materials and in various settings to make sure it looks great and works well for your brand.

- Stay consistent: once you've found the perfect colour palette, use it consistently across all your branding materials. This will help create a cohesive look and make your brand easy to recognise.

What about typography?

This one is for all you font fans out there! I have to admit that I have a slight font addiction; I'm always looking for the perfect font and have a sizable collection of fonts for my designs. So let's talk about the magic of typography. Picking the right fonts is like adding the perfect finishing touch to your brand's style. Let's dive into the world of typography and explore how to find the best fonts that match your brand's personality and make it look fantastic!

Why Typography Matters

Typography is more than just words on a page—it's a powerful design element that can make your brand stand out. Here's why typography is so important:

- It sets the tone and voice of your brand.

- It communicates your brand's personality.

- It makes your brand easy to read and understand.

- It helps you stand out from the competition.

- It creates a visual hierarchy and guides readers through your content.

Understanding Font Styles

There are so many fonts out there, it can be a little overwhelming! But don't worry, let's start by looking at some common font styles and what they say about your brand:

- Serif: classic, traditional, trustworthy

- Sans-serif: modern, clean, minimal

- Script: elegant, creative, personal

- Display: bold, attention-grabbing, unique

Choosing Your Font Style

- Know your brand's personality: before you start browsing fonts, think about your brand's personality, values, and target audience. This will help you choose fonts that feel just right for your brand.

- Look for inspiration: keep your eyes open for typography inspiration everywhere you go! Look at other brands, design trends, and even your favourite books and magazines to find fonts that speak to you.

- Pick a primary font: choose a main font that captures the essence of your brand. This font will be used for headlines, titles, and other important text.

- Select a secondary font: find a secondary font that complements your primary font. This font will be used for body text, captions, and other smaller text.

- Consider readability: make sure your chosen fonts are easy to read and understand. You want your audience to be able to quickly and effortlessly read your content.

- Test your typography: try out your typography choices on different materials and in various settings to make sure they look great and work well for your brand.

- Stay consistent: once you've found the perfect typography, use it consistently across all your branding materials. This will help create a cohesive look and make your brand easy to recognise.

Choosing the right typography for your brand is like putting the cherry on top of a delicious cake—it's the perfect finishing touch! By understanding the importance of typography, learning about font styles, and following a step-by-step guide, you can create a typography style that truly brings your brand to life.

Finding the Right Imagery for Your Brand

The right images can truly make your brand come alive and create a strong connection with your audience. Let's explore how to find the perfect imagery that reflects your brand's personality and makes it look absolutely fabulous!

1. **Why imagery matters**

Imagery is like the icing on your brand's cake—it adds flavour, depth, and excitement. Here's why imagery is so important:

- It tells your brand's story in a visual way.

- It captures your audience's attention.

- It evokes emotions and creates a mood.

- It helps you stand out from the competition.

- It adds personality and life to your brand.

2. Types of Imagery

There are lots of different types of imagery you can use to bring your brand to life. Here are some popular options to consider:

- Photography: high-quality photos that showcase your products, services, or brand's lifestyle

- Illustrations: unique, hand-drawn images that add a personal touch to your brand

- Icons: simple, stylized images that represent ideas, concepts, or actions.

- Infographics: visual representations of data or information that make it easy to understand

- Patterns and textures: repeating images or designs that add depth and interest to your branding materials

3. Choosing Your Brand's Imagery: A Step-by-Step Guide

a) Understand your brand's personality: before you start hunting for images, think about your brand's personality, values, and target audience. This will help you choose imagery that feels just right for your brand.

b) Look for inspiration: keep your eyes open for imagery inspiration everywhere you go! Look at other brands, design trends, and even your favourite movies and TV shows to find images that speak to you.

c) Pick a style: choose an imagery style that matches your brand's personality and vibe. This could be anything from bright, bold photography to whimsical, hand-drawn illustrations.

d) Be consistent: make sure your chosen imagery style is consistent across all your branding materials. This will help create a cohesive look and make your brand easy to recognise.

e) Use high-quality images: it's important to use high-quality, professional-looking images for your brand. Blurred, pixelated, or poorly lit images can make your brand look unprofessional and unappealing.

f) Consider your audience: keep your target audience in mind when choosing imagery. Make sure the images you use resonate with them and reflect their values, interests, and lifestyle.

g) Test your imagery: try out your imagery choices on different materials and in various settings to make sure they look great and work well for your brand.

Finding the right imagery for your brand is like adding a splash of colour and excitement to your brand's canvas—it brings your brand to life and creates a strong connection with your audience. By understanding the importance of imagery, exploring different types, and following the step-by-step guide, you can create an imagery style that truly captures your brand's essence.

Guiding Your Style: How a Style Guide Boosts Your Branding Game

Ever heard of a style guide? It's like a trusty roadmap that helps you navigate the world of branding and keep your style on point. Let's uncover the magic of style guides and explore how they can help you create a cohesive, memorable brand that shines!

1. What is a style guide?

A style guide is your brand's best friend—it's a handy document that outlines your brand's visual and messaging elements, such as colours, typography, imagery, and tone of voice. A style guide helps you:

- Keep your branding consistent across different platforms and materials.

- Create a cohesive look and feel for your brand.

- Make it easy for you and your team to create on-brand content.

- Ensure your brand is instantly recognisable and memorable.

2. Key Components of a Style Guide

A well-crafted style guide includes everything you need to make your brand look fabulous and stay consistent. Here are the main components of a great style guide:

- Logo: include your logo in different formats and sizes, along with guidelines for how to use it.

- Colour palette: list your brand's primary and secondary colours, along with their colour codes (e.g., RGB, CMYK, or HEX).

- Typography: showcase your brand's primary and secondary fonts, along with guidelines for their usage (e.g., headings, body text, etc.).

- Imagery: outline the types of imagery you use (e.g., photography, illustrations, icons), and provide examples of on-brand images.

- Tone of voice: describe your brand's messaging style, along with tips for writing in that style (e.g., friendly, formal, playful).

- Layouts and templates: provide templates for common materials, such as business cards, social media posts, or email signatures.

3. Creating Your Brand's Style Guide: A Step-by-Step Guide

a) Gather inspiration: look at other brands' style guides for inspiration and ideas. This can help you get a feel for what works well and what you'd like to include in your own style guide. A quick Google search for 'style guide examples' should help you.

b) Organise your elements: make a list of all the visual and messaging elements you want to include in your style guide (e.g., logo, colours, fonts, etc.).

c) Be detailed: for each element, provide clear guidelines and examples of how it should be used. This will make it easy for anyone working with your brand to create consistent, on-brand content.

d) Make it easy to follow: keep your style guide simple, organised, and easy to understand. Use clear headings, bullet points, and visual examples to make it user-friendly.

e) Update regularly: as your brand evolves, make sure to update your style guide with any new elements or changes. This will help keep your brand looking fresh and cohesive.

A style guide is like your brand's secret weapon—it helps you create a consistent, cohesive, and memorable brand that truly stands out. By understanding the importance of a style guide, learning about its key components, and following the step-by-step guide, you can create a style guide that keeps your brand looking fabulous and on track.

Dipping Our Toes into the World of Book Cover Design and Branding

Welcome to this delightful little section, where we'll explore the fascinating realm of book cover design as an integral part of your brand's visual identity. We've already learned about the significance of branding for your entire business, and now it's time to see how it relates to your book covers. While this is a vast subject, we won't be able to dive deep into every aspect within these pages. Instead, consider this a useful starting point for your book cover branding adventure.

Let's discuss how branding influences your book designs and the ways you can harness its power. The concepts we've covered in this chapter can now be applied to your book covers as well.

First things first, let's chat about colours. Choosing the right colours for your book cover is a vital part of creating an appealing brand. Colours can convey emotions and set the tone for your book. For instance, warm colours like red or orange can evoke feelings of passion or excitement, while cooler tones like blue or green might convey calmness or trustworthiness. A romance novel might use hues of red or pink to depict love, while a thriller might opt for darker shades to set a suspenseful mood. Even non-fiction and low-content books need to carefully consider colour choice. A self-help book might use warm and inviting colours to convey positivity, while a planner could use neutral tones for a clean, organised look.

Remember, these are just suggestions; the best colour for your book cover is the one that accurately reflects your content and appeals to your target audience. For my own branding as an author of 'The Home Boss Toolkit: Mastering Branding for Self-Publishers', I've chosen a primary palette of navy blue and white, signifying trust and clarity, with a secondary accent of golden yellow, symbolising wisdom and wealth. This colour scheme continues in the accompanying workbook, though with a lighter blue and vibrant green, making it more approachable and signifying growth.

Such thoughtful colour selection is not a random process; it's part of creating a consistent visual language - your style guide. A style guide, as we've discussed earlier, is the roadmap for your brand. It lays out the visual and stylistic choices that will represent your brand across different platforms and materials. Your style guide would include specific colour codes, fonts, imagery guidelines, and even the tone of your writing.

To create your style guide, you need to start by understanding your brand's personality and how you want to convey it to your readers. You then choose elements that mirror this personality. It's a fun and creative process, but it also requires some reflection and strategic thinking.

In the workbook accompanying 'The Home Boss Toolkit', there are practical exercises designed to guide you through creating your own style guide. For instance, there is a colour emotion guide that you can use to understand the kinds of feelings different colours might evoke. By understanding this, you can make more informed decisions when selecting a colour palette that will work best for your brand.

This exploration into the world of branding for self-publishers is not just about adding aesthetic value. It is about creating a unique identity, building recognition, and connecting with your readers on a deeper level. Remember, your brand is not just what people see; it's what people feel when they interact with your work. So, choose your colours wisely, be consistent, and most importantly, let your brand tell your story.

Now, onto typography.

The choice of typography can indeed play a significant role in conveying the genre and mood of your book. Here's a brief rundown:

Serif fonts, which have little "feet" or lines attached to the ends of their letters, are often associated with more traditional, serious, or academic works. They're commonly used for literary fiction, historical fiction, or non-fiction. An example of a widely used serif font is Times New Roman.

Sans Serif fonts, meaning "without serif," are seen as modern, clean, and straightforward. They're a popular choice for business and self-help books, as well as contemporary fiction. Arial and Helvetica are two well-known Sans Serif fonts.

Script fonts, which resemble handwriting or calligraphy, can communicate elegance, creativity, or a personal touch. They're often used for romance novels, poetry books, or titles in the creative non-fiction genre.

Display fonts are usually unique and eye-catching. These fonts can range in style and are used when a strong visual impact is desired. They can be suitable for children's books, fantasy, sci-fi, or any genre where the author wants to project a unique, individualised identity.

Remember, though, that these are not strict rules. The beauty of typography lies in its ability to be manipulated and used creatively to create the right visual cue for your book. It's about finding a balance between what's appropriate for your genre and what truly represents your individual book and author brand. It's always a good idea to look at successful books within your genre for inspiration, but don't be afraid to think outside the box and experiment to find a font that fits your unique vision.

Choosing the right fonts is essential for crafting a brand that reflects your unique personality. Opt for one or two easy-to-read fonts that harmonise with your cover designs, and make sure to use them consistently across your marketing materials. Typography, much like colour, plays a crucial role in communicating your book's genre and setting the right tone. The font you choose becomes the voice of your book on its cover. Serif fonts often give off a traditional or classic vibe, while sans-serif fonts look modern and clean. Cursive or script fonts might suggest elegance or creativity, and display fonts can be used to make a bold and distinctive statement. It's important to choose a font that not only aligns with your book's content but is also easily legible, even at thumbnail size.

Next, we'll tackle imagery and illustrations. The visuals on your book covers should align with the overall atmosphere of your brand. Imagery and illustrations play a crucial role in defining your book cover's personality. They form the visual vocabulary that communicates your book's mood, tone, and content to potential readers. Just like colours and typography, images and illustrations should also align with your brand's style and your target audience's preferences.

For instance, a light-hearted romance novel may benefit from playful, dreamy illustrations, while a hard-hitting investigative journalism book might need impactful, realistic imagery. Remember, your cover image should resonate with the story inside your book and the expectations of your genre's readers.

Your brand's tone and style should also inform your book design choices. The tone and style of your book cover serve as your novel's first impression, subtly communicating the genre, mood, and essence of your story to potential readers. It's all about creating an emotional resonance that aligns with your story's content and your brand identity.

For instance, if your brand is all about delivering gritty, fast-paced thrillers, your cover style should mirror this with intense, striking visuals and bold typography. However, if you're a romance novelist known for heartwarming, tender tales, a softer, dreamy aesthetic with elegant fonts would be more fitting.

The task then is to find the tone and style that best encapsulate your brand's personality, your book's genre, and your readers' expectations.

Consistency is crucial, particularly if you're writing books within a specific genre or series. Aim for a cohesive appearance in your book designs, making it easy for readers to recognise your work and feel a sense of familiarity when they spot your books.

Last but not least, remember your **logo or author name.** A unique logo or consistent presentation of your author name on your book covers and promotional materials strengthens your brand identity, making your work effortlessly recognisable and fostering trust with your readers.

The way you showcase your brand through your book designs can significantly impact how readers perceive and connect with your work. By focusing on elements like colours, typography, imagery, tone, and consistency, you can establish a powerful brand that resonates with your target audience and sets you apart in the self-publishing world. And most importantly, have fun with it and let your creative spirit soar!

"Let your visual identity be the vibrant canvas that paints your brand's story for the world to see."

Chapter Eight

Building your Digital Empire

Your Brand's Online Presence

I'm thrilled you made it this far and are ready to take a dive into the world of branding. Now, we're about to tackle a pivotal part of your journey—building your digital brand. What is it, you might ask? Let's put it in the simplest terms possible. Your digital brand is your reputation, your image, and your 'signature' in the vast online world. It's how readers perceive you and your books across digital platforms, whether that be on your website, Amazon, or social media. You could also say that a brand's digital presence is its online representation across various platforms, such as websites, social media profiles, email marketing campaigns, and other digital channels. It's how a brand showcases itself, connects with customers, and conducts business online. A consistent image and message are vital for establishing credibility, building trust, connecting with customers, increasing visibility, and ultimately driving sales.

As a self-published author, having a robust digital presence is essential for reaching new readers and growing your business.

Understanding the Key Components

There are four key components we're going to explore in detail in the coming chapters, but let's do a brief overview now. These four pillars of your digital brand are:

1. Amazon Author Central Account

2. A Website

3. Social media for promotion

4. Email Marketing

Your Amazon Author Central account is your home on the world's largest book marketplace. It's where readers get to know more about you and your work. Here, you can showcase your books and let your readers know more about you.

Your website, on the other hand, is your personal corner of the internet, where you can showcase your books, share updates, and engage your readers in a more personal, intimate way. It's a hub for your digital brand, and it's a place where all your branding elements converge and interact harmoniously.

Social media is your loudspeaker. It's where you shout from the digital rooftops about your latest book release, share snippets of your writing process, and build a community of loyal fans who can't wait to read your next book.

Lastly, email marketing is your direct line to your readers. It's a more private, more personal channel where you can share exclusive content, updates, and offers that your subscribers will love.

A Sneak Peek at What's to Come

We're going to dive deeper into each of these key areas in the upcoming chapters. We'll look at the nuts and bolts of setting up and managing an Amazon Author Central account, designing an engaging author website, harnessing the power of social media for book promotion, and making the most out of email marketing to nurture your reader relationships.

I understand that it might sound a tad overwhelming at this point, but I promise you, it's going to be an exciting ride. With a bit of planning and step-by-step execution, you'll be well on your way to building a robust digital brand that resonates with your readers and boosts your book sales.

So, dear author, brace yourself! You're about to transform from a 'writer' to a 'brand.' Welcome to the wonderful world of branding for self-publishers.

Stay tuned for the next chapter, where we deep dive into the first component, the Amazon Author Central Account.

Let's make some branding magic!

Your Amazon Author Central Account

In the self-publishing universe, Amazon Author Central is your secret weapon. Not only is it a free tool, but it's like your own virtual home on the world's biggest online book marketplace. If there's only one action you take as an author to build your digital brand, make it creating an Amazon Author Central account.

Amazon Author Central allows you to establish your Author Page, your personal corner on Amazon, where you can share the most current information about yourself and your books with millions of readers worldwide. It's the beacon that helps readers discover and connect with your work, creating a one-stop-shop for all your titles.

What can you do with your Author Central Account?

You can

     1. Add Your Books

     2. Craft Your Biography

     3. Add Photos and Videos

     4. Track Your Progress

     5. Add Editorial Reviews

6. Check Sales Information

One of the most engaging features of Amazon Author Central is the 'Author Follow' option. This lets your fans add you to their list of favourite authors. When they follow you, they're notified about your new book releases or pre-order availability, provided they allow marketing emails from Amazon and haven't already ordered your new book.

Your number of followers doesn't affect your Amazon Best Sellers Rank, but it does enhance your community of readers and increases the chances of your new releases being seen while browsing on Amazon.

To sum it up, Amazon Author Central is an indispensable tool in your author branding arsenal. It amplifies your presence on Amazon and allows you to understand and connect with your readers more effectively. If you want to boost your visibility and credibility as a self-published author, this is one step you simply can't skip.

Setting Up and Optimising Your Amazon Author Central Account

Now that you understand the value of having an Amazon Author Central account, let's dive into the nitty-gritty details of setting it up and optimising it to its fullest potential.

Setting up your Amazon Author Central account is straightforward and can be done in a few simple steps. Here's how:

1. **Access Author Central:** Log in to your Kindle Direct Publishing (KDP) account and go to the Marketing page.

2. **Select Your Marketplace:** In the Author Central section, choose the marketplace where you'd like to create your author page from the drop-down menu. As of now, Amazon Author Central supports the following marketplaces: Amazon.com, Amazon.co.uk, Amazon.de, Amazon.fr, Amazon.co.jp, and Amazon.com.br.

3. **Create Your Account:** Click on 'Manage author page.' You'll be redirected to Author Central. Click 'Join for free' and use your KDP account information to sign up.

Congratulations! You have created your Amazon Author Central account. But the journey doesn't end here. Now comes the part where we optimise your author page to make it compelling and attractive for readers.

1. **Add Your Books:** Start by adding all your books to your author page. This will create a comprehensive list of all your works, making it easy for your readers to find and purchase them.

2. **Craft a Compelling Bio:** Your biography is a powerful tool to connect with your readers on a personal level. Write a compelling, authentic bio that gives readers an insight into who you are and what inspires your writing. Remember, you can write this bio in multiple languages to connect with international readers. More on that later.

3. **Add High-Quality Photos and Videos:** If you're a non-US author, make sure to take advantage of the opportunity to add photos and videos. This can provide a more engaging experience for your readers and give them a glimpse into your world. Ensure the photos and videos are professional and high-quality.

4. **Monitor Your Progress:** Regularly check your Amazon Best Sellers Rank and customer reviews to understand how your books are performing. Use this information to adjust your marketing and writing strategies as needed.

5. **Leverage Editorial Reviews:** If you're a US author, don't forget to add editorial reviews to your books. They add credibility to your work and can influence potential readers to buy your books.

Remember, your Amazon Author Central account is not a 'set it and forget it' tool. Regular updates and interactions are key to making the most of it. Keep your bio, photos, and book list up-to-date.

Crafting a Compelling Author Bio

Your author bio is more than just a brief summary of who you are. It's an opportunity to connect with your readers on a personal level and give them a sense of what you and your writing are all about. A well-crafted bio can intrigue your readers, make you more relatable, and ultimately drive more interest in your books.

Here are some tips for creating an engaging author bio:

1. **Keep it Relevant:** Start by sharing a little about yourself, including any relevant experiences or qualifications that relate to your genre or the types of books you write. This can help establish your credibility and relevance in your field.

2. **Share Personal Details (Thoughtfully):** Adding a personal touch can make your bio more engaging. You might mention where you live, your hobbies, or fun facts about yourself. However, only share what you're comfortable with—your privacy is important.

3. **Speak to Your Readers:** Try to write from the perspective of what a reader might find interesting or compelling. What would you want to know about an author whose books you enjoy?

4. **Stay Professional:** Even though you're sharing personal details, it's important to maintain a professional tone. Keep your bio clear, concise, and free of errors.

5. **Update Regularly:** Make sure to update your bio from time to time, especially when you release a new book or achieve a significant milestone.

Remember, your bio is often a reader's first introduction to you as an author, so make it count. Let your personality shine through, and you'll be well on your way to creating a meaningful connection with your readers.

If you're struggling to create your author bio, here is a step-by-step worksheet that you can use to craft your author bio. Take a moment to fill out each section. Try to be concise, aiming for a final bio of 100–150 words (a short bio) or up to 300 words (a long bio). Once you have your draft, take some time to revise and polish it. Also, look at other writers' bios to find inspiration and examples. Remember to update it regularly as your career progresses and you have new information to share. Happy writing!

Author Bio Creation Worksheet

Step 1: Identify Your Key Information

- Name (as it appears on your books)

- Genre(s) you write in

- Number of books you've published

- Any writing credentials or relevant professional experiences

Step 2: Personal Background

- Where are you from, or where do you currently reside?

- What personal experiences influenced your writing?

- What hobbies or interests do you have outside of writing?

Step 3: Connect with Your Readers

Think about what your readers might find interesting about you and your writing. How can you show them that you're not just an author but also a person they can relate to?

Step 4: Showcase Your Achievements

If you've received any awards or recognitions for your writing, list them here. Don't be shy about sharing your achievements; they add credibility to your author brand.

Step 5: Update Your Information

What's the most recent significant thing you've done? Have you just released a new book, started a new series, or hit a milestone in your writing career?

Author biographies for publishing brands and low-content book creators

But what if your brand is a publishing brand rather than an author brand? What if you create low-content books? How could you write a good author bio? Crafting a bio for a publishing brand or for a creator of low-content books might require a slightly different approach. Your focus should be less on personal details and more on the unique value that your books provide. Here's how to adjust the steps from the previous exercise:

Step 1: Identify Your Key Information

- Name of your brand or publishing entity

- Types of books you publish (e.g., journals, colouring books, planners, etc.)

- Number of books you've published or the breadth of your collection

Step 2: The Mission of Your Brand

- What is your brand's mission or vision?

- What sets your brand or books apart from others in the market?

- What values or principles does your brand stand for?

Step 3: Connect With Your Customers

- What benefits do your customers gain from your products?

- How do your books enhance their lifestyle or productivity?

- Why should they choose your books over others?

Step 4: Showcase Your Achievements

- If your brand or books have received any awards, recognitions, or notable reviews, mention them here.

- Share if you've achieved high sales numbers, ranking positions, or other milestones.

Step 5: Update Your Information

- Have you recently expanded your collection?

- Have you launched a new line of books or entered a new market segment?

The aim here is to position your brand as a reliable, high-quality source for the type of low-content books you produce. Make sure your bio reflects the unique value proposition of your brand and how it serves your customers. Just as with an author bio, try to keep it concise and remember to update it regularly as your brand grows and evolves.

Your Author Photo

What kind of author photo should you use? For an individual author, the photo is typically a professional headshot that presents the author in a positive and approachable light. The choice of clothing, background, and overall style of the photo may reflect the genre or tone of the author's works. For instance, a thriller writer might choose a more intense, dramatic photo, while a children's book author might opt for a brighter, more whimsical image.

For a low-content book creator or a publishing brand, a personal headshot might not be the most relevant or effective choice, particularly if the brand is not closely tied to a single individual. Instead, you might consider the following alternatives:

1. **Logo**: If your brand has a distinctive logo, using that as your author photo can help increase brand recognition. Make sure the logo is clear and high-resolution.

2. **Book Collage**: A collage or montage of your book covers can showcase the variety and style of your products, appealing directly to the interests of your potential customers.

3. **Thematic Image**: If your brand has a strong theme or a consistent aesthetic (for example, if you create a lot of nature-themed colouring books), a high-quality, visually striking image that represents this theme can be a good choice.

4. **Illustration or Graphic**: An illustration or graphic image that reflects the spirit and values of your brand can also work well. This could be a character from your books, an abstract design, or any other visual that conveys the feel of your brand.

In all cases, the image you choose should be high-quality and professional-looking. It should also comply with any guidelines or restrictions set by the platform you're using (for example, Amazon Author Central).

Closing thoughts

To wrap this all up, having an Amazon Author Central account is really like holding a magic key to unlocking your brand's potential on Amazon. It's the place where you can show your readers who you are, both as an author and a publisher, and make your books shine in their very best light. Crafting an engaging author bio and choosing just the right photo? These are like the cherries on top of your brand's cake.

And let me tell you, that little 'Author Follow' button can be an absolute game changer. I've personally seen it work wonders on my book sales, especially for those books where I don't have a separate email list. Picture this: every time you've got a new release, your followers get notified. It's like having a dedicated group of readers just waiting to dive into your next book. How awesome is that?

So don't let the opportunity slip through your fingers. Set up and maintain your Amazon Author Central account. It's not rocket science, but it's definitely a move that can help propel your brand into the limelight. Trust me, it's a small step that could lead to giant leaps in building your brand and boosting your sales. You've got this!

Your Brand Website

A hub for your brand

Let's dive right into our next big chapter: The Author Website. If there's one place where all the magic happens, where everything about you and your books comes together in a symphony of branding, it's your author website. Picture this: Your website is like the bustling city centre of your self-publishing business. It's vibrant, informative, engaging, and most importantly, it's all about you and your books.

Now, you may wonder, "Why do I need a website when I've got my Amazon Author Central page?" Good question! Here's the thing: an Amazon Author Central page is more like a cosy little bookshop showcasing your books, but your website? It's like your open, inviting home, where readers can pop in, look around, and really get to know you and your brand.

A good author website is easy to navigate, professional, and offers valuable information about you and your books. It's where you can go beyond the basic book descriptions and author bio, and truly connect with your readers. Share your writing journey, give sneak peeks into your upcoming books, discuss your inspiration, and so much more. It's your playground, so make it as personal and engaging as you want!

Now, let's get practical. Building a website can feel a little daunting if you've never done it before, but don't worry; it's easier than you think. Platforms like Podia, Payhip, Wix, or Squarespace are user-friendly and offer plenty of sleek, professional templates to get you started. Remember, you don't need to be a tech whiz to build an effective author website. It's all about making it a welcoming space for your readers.

Think about the essentials: an 'About' page, a 'Books' page, a 'Contact' page, and maybe a 'Blog' page if you're up for regular blogging. And, of course, make sure there's a clear, easy way for visitors to sign up for your email newsletter.

As for the look and feel of your website, this is where your branding comes into play. Be consistent with your colour scheme, fonts, and images to ensure they reflect your author or publishing brand.

Remember, your author website isn't just a fancy addition to your self-publishing toolkit; it's the hub of your online presence and a powerful way to build your brand. It's time to roll up your sleeves and create a home for your books online. Trust me, you've got this!

Let's deep-dive into **the nitty-gritty details** of an author website and explore how it might differ if you're focusing on an author brand, publishing brand or low-content books. Remember, we're in this together, and I'm here to make this as simple and fun as possible. So grab a cup of tea or coffee, and let's get started.

Whether you're an author or a publisher, there are a few essential components that every good website should have. Here are the top five:

1. **Home Page:** This is the first page visitors see when they land on your website. Make it inviting and easy to navigate. Think of it like your living room: you want guests to feel welcome and intrigued enough to explore further.

2. **About Page:** This is your chance to introduce yourself and share your story. If you're an author, talk about your writing journey, your inspirations, and maybe even a few fun facts. If you're a publishing brand or low-content book creator, discuss your company's mission, your approach to creating books, and why you love what you do.

3. **Books Page:** Showcase your books! If you're an author, include beautiful cover images, enticing descriptions, and clear links to where readers can buy them. If you're a publishing brand, you might want to categorise your books by genre or type of content. In either case, make it easy for visitors to browse and get excited about your books.

4. **Contact Page:** Make it simple for readers, potential collaborators, or the press to reach out to you. A basic form, or your email address, should suffice.

5. **Newsletter Sign-Up:** This is a must-have! It's your way to collect email addresses from interested readers who want to hear more from you. Offer them something in return, like exclusive news, discounts, or a freebie. More on this later.

Now, here's where things might differ slightly if you're creating low-content books or running a publishing company. Instead of personal blog posts about your writing process or character development, you might want to focus on blog posts about your publishing process, tips for using your low-content books, or features about your authors. The key is to think about what your target audience will find interesting and valuable.

Remember, your website isn't a static thing. It's a living, breathing part of your brand that you can (and should) regularly update and improve. Don't stress about making it "perfect" right away. The most important thing is to get started and refine as you go. I know it might seem like a lot right now, but once you've got the basic structure down, everything else will fall into place. So, are you ready to take the plunge? I promise it'll be worth it!

Getting Started: Breaking Down the Basics

If you're new to website building, terms like domain names, hosting platforms, and website builder might seem intimidating and confusing. Let's think of it like a fun puzzle we're solving together. It might look a bit confusing at first, but with a little patience, all the pieces will come together. Ready? Okay, let's go!

1. **Domain Name:** Think of your domain name as your home address on the internet. It's the web address that people type into their browsers to find your website. Ideally, your domain name should be your name or your publishing company's name, like "YourName.com" or "YourPublishingCompany.com". You can buy your domain from domain registrars like GoDaddy, Namecheap, or Google Domains.

2. **Hosting Platform:** Your hosting platform is like the plot of land where your internet "house" (website) is built. It's where all your website files (like text, photos, and videos) live. There are many hosting platforms to choose from, but some popular ones are Bluehost, SiteGround, and Dreamhost. Look for one that fits your budget, is easy to use, and has good customer support.

3. **Website Builder:** A website builder is your construction crew. It's the tool you use to design and build your website. WordPress is a highly customizable website builder loved by many, but it can be a bit complex for beginners. Squarespace, Wix, and Weebly are more user-friendly, and they offer gorgeous, ready-to-use templates.

Now let's connect the dots. Once you've chosen your domain name and bought it from a registrar, the next step is to pick a hosting platform. After purchasing a hosting plan, you'll link it to your domain name (the hosting platform will guide you on how to do this). With your "land" and "address" all set, you can start building! Choose a website builder that you feel comfortable with, pick a template you love, and then start adding your content (like your about page, books page, and contact page).

Don't worry if it feels overwhelming at first. You're learning a whole new language here, and it's completely okay to take it slow. And remember, there's always help out there! You can hire a web developer or designer if you're feeling stuck or overwhelmed. But I believe in you! You're taking big, brave steps to create your online home, and I'm cheering you on every step of the way. Ready for the next piece of the puzzle? Let's go!

Where should I start?

So, let's dive into a little storytelling. Ready?

Once upon a time (just kidding), when I embarked on this digital journey of setting up my website, I, like many others, gravitated towards Word-Press. It's a popular choice, after all, and it's famous for its customizability and versatility. WordPress is like the Swiss Army knife of website builders; there's a tool for everything! However, it can be a bit of a tough cookie to crack if you're new to the world of website building, and I certainly felt that.

For me, learning WordPress felt a bit like learning a new language. I spent many a late night wrestling with widgets, tangling with templates, and grappling with plugins. Oh, the plugins! They're super helpful tools that can add just about any feature you can think of to your website. But they can also be a bit tricky to master, especially when you're just starting out.

While I'm grateful for all I learned through my WordPress experience, I started to wonder if there might be an easier way. And guess what? I found two! I now use Podia and Payhip, and they're like a breath of fresh air.

Podia and Payhip are straightforward and user-friendly. I've found their interfaces to be intuitive and easy to navigate. In other words, you won't need to go on late-night Google expeditions to figure out how to use them. And they also host your site, so no need for a host and a separate website builder, everything is in one place.

With Podia by my side, I've been able to bring my digital products, memberships, and even email marketing all under one cosy digital roof. Talk about a game-changer! On the other hand, Payhip has swept in like a cool breeze, making the sale of my eBooks and digital downloads as effortless as a Sunday morning. And the cherry on top? They both come with built-in marketing tools like discounts, affiliates, and even pay-what-you-want pricing, not to mention the fabulous customer support they offer!

Now, I wouldn't want to play favourites and say which one is better, because they're a bit like apples and oranges—similar in some ways, but each with their own unique flavour. So, it's really all about finding the one that's the best fit for you. Remember, this is just a snippet from my own digital adventure, and your journey might look a bit different. So, do some exploring, dig into the features each platform offers, and find the one that suits your taste the best. After all, building your website should feel just right for you!

Keep in mind that every journey is unique. My path led me from WordPress to Podia and Payhip, but yours might look a little different. And that's perfectly fine! Remember, the best tools are the ones that serve your specific needs and make your life easier. It's all about finding what works for you.

In this digital adventure, there's always something new to learn and a new path to explore. And while the journey might seem daunting at times, trust me, it's totally worth it. So, strap on your adventure boots, because you're building something great! Ready to continue? Let's go!

The Finishing Touches to Your Author Website

Alrighty, we've spent some good time chatting about the building blocks of your author website—the purpose, the content, the platforms, you name it! But just like the perfect cup of coffee, it's all in the details. Let's delve into some finer points that can truly make your website stand out in the crowd and provide an inviting, memorable space for your readers.

- **Mobile Friendliness:** Did you know that over half of the global web traffic comes from mobile devices? You heard that right! So, it's crucial that your website looks great and functions well not just on a desktop but on mobile devices too. A mobile-friendly design ensures your readers can comfortably browse your website, no matter what device they're using.

- **Easy Navigation:** Think of your website like your readers' personal tour guide to your work. Make it easy for them to find what they're looking for with simple, intuitive navigation. A clearly labelled menu, an easy-to-find contact page, and an accessible search feature can work wonders!

- **Contact Form:** Don't forget to include a way for your readers to get in touch with you! A simple contact form is a great way to invite comments, questions, or even requests for interviews or book signings.

- **Links to Retailers:** If you're selling your books through online retailers, make sure to include direct links on your website. Make the purchasing process as easy as possible for your readers.

- **Blog:** If you're up for it, maintaining a blog can be a wonderful way to connect with your readers on a more personal level. Share updates, behind-the-scenes sneak peeks, or even posts about your writing process. Just remember, a blog is like a pet—it needs regular care and feeding!

- **Testimonials and Reviews:** Let your satisfied readers do the talking. Showcasing glowing testimonials or reviews on your website can convince potential readers that your book is worth their time.

- **Author Newsletter Signup:** Finally, don't forget about your email list! Include a simple signup form on your website to keep your readers in the loop about your upcoming works, book signings, or any other exciting news.

Remember, your website is an extension of your brand as an author. It's a little corner of the internet that is all yours. Let it reflect your personality, your passion, and your unique voice. With these finishing touches, you'll be well on your way to creating a truly engaging author website that readers will love to visit!

Learning from the Best: What Existing Author Websites Can Teach You About Building Your Own

One of my strategies that I often use for my business is to take a look at my competition. And I don't just do this for website ideas; I use this tactic for a lot of my business decisions. If you're unsure where to start or what elements to include in your website, why not learn from the best?

Ever heard the saying, "Imitation is the sincerest form of flattery?" Well, when it comes to creating your author website, there's absolutely no shame in drawing inspiration from those who've already walked the path. You don't need to reinvent the wheel. There's a lot to learn from the successes (and maybe even the missteps) of existing author websites. So grab a cup of your favourite brew, and let's play the role of website detectives for a moment.

1. Engaging Visuals: Visit the websites of authors you admire. Pay attention to the visuals. Do they use a certain colour palette? Is there a unique style or mood to their photos? Note down what appeals to you visually. Remember, your website should reflect your brand and genre, so consider how you can adapt these visual cues to fit your own unique style.

2. Website Structure: Look at how these websites are organised. Where is the navigation menu located? How many pages do they have, and what are they? Is it easy to find what you're looking for? The structure of your website can greatly impact a visitor's experience, so make a note of what works and what doesn't!

3. Author Bio: Read through a few author bios. What kind of information do they include? How do they introduce themselves? An author bio is your chance to connect with your readers on a personal level, so look for elements you could incorporate into your own bio.

4. Book Pages: Examine the pages dedicated to the authors' books. What information do they provide? Do they include book covers, blurbs, reviews, and buying options? Consider what you could include on your own book pages.

5. Contact Options: How do these authors allow readers to contact them? Do they have a contact form, an email address, or social media links? Remember, enabling your readers to reach out to you easily is essential.

6. Extra Features: Last but not least, keep an eye out for any extra features that stand out. Do they have a blog? Do they offer a newsletter? Perhaps they have a 'Press' page with interviews and articles? These extra features can provide additional value to your readers and keep them coming back.

Remember, the goal here isn't to copy these websites verbatim. It's to learn from them, to take inspiration, and then to put your own unique spin on things. After all, your website should be as unique as you are. But with these tips in mind, you'll have a solid foundation to build your author website on.

And remember how we talked about learning from the best? Well, the most successful author websites have a little secret: they're always bustling with activity! They keep their readers hooked by consistently dishing out fresh content and the latest news. So when you're piecing together your own author website, think about how you can keep that same kind of energy going.

Maybe you could start a blog and regularly share snippets from your writing journey. Or, you could keep your readers in the loop about any upcoming book signings, readings, or other events you're participating in. And don't forget to celebrate your successes! Whenever you have a new release, make sure it gets the spotlight on your book list! Remember, your website isn't just a static advertisement; it's a dynamic, evolving part of your author brand. So keep it fresh, exciting, and uniquely you!

Your Website, Your Goldmine for Starting an Email List

We've been on quite the journey so far, haven't we? Building an awesome website, making it the heart of your author brand, and keeping it alive with fresh and exciting content. But guess what? There's even more treasure to be found here! Yes, your website is the perfect place to start an email list.

Now, I hear you asking, "Why on earth would I want to start collecting emails?" Let me tell you, an email list is one of the most powerful tools in your author arsenal. Think of it like a direct line to your readers. Unlike social media, where your posts can get lost in the sea of other content, emails land right in your readers' inboxes, ready to be opened and read at their leisure.

Through your emails, you can share updates, send out reminders about your new releases, offer sneak peeks, or offer special discounts. Even better? Those on your email list are typically your most dedicated fans; they want to hear from you!

And where does your website fit into all of this? Well, it's the perfect gathering spot! You can have a simple sign-up form on your website where interested readers can join your email list. But hold on; we'll dive deep into the nuts and bolts of email marketing in an upcoming chapter. For now, just remember: Your website isn't only about showcasing you and your books; it's also a launchpad for building your community of readers via your email list. Cool, right?

"Social media isn't just about likes and followers; it's about creating meaningful connections and empowering others through your words and actions."

Unlock The Power Of Email

Building A Loyal Fan Base

Why is building an email list so important for authors?

The secret weapon in your author's arsenal? An email list. I can't emphasise this enough: building a solid email list is like planting a sapling that, with time and attention, will grow into a flourishing tree, strengthening the roots of your publishing venture. And it's your job to nurture it.

You might ask, "Why can't I just rely on social media?" Good question! Social media is indeed a vital player in your promotional strategy, but it's not your only team member. Let's explore why an email list can be an author's best friend.

Here's a game-changer: Your email list is yours to keep. There are no changing algorithms or sudden platform policies that can make your visibility vanish like a magic trick. Your email list is your direct line to your readers. And no matter what the social media landscape looks like, your email list remains untouched and always within your control. Remember, your social media followers belong to that platform, but your email list? It's exclusively yours!

Another bonus point for email lists is the opportunity to cultivate more profound relationships with your readers. With the constant buzz of content on social media platforms, personal connections often get lost. Emails, however, offer a more intimate, distraction-free channel. It's like a personal letter landing in your reader's inbox, allowing you to share updates, personal stories, and exclusive offers. This one-to-one communication nurtures trust and strengthens your bond with your audience.

Emails give you the ability to fine-tune your marketing strategy. By keeping an eye on your email metrics, you can understand what content resonates with your readers, enabling you to tailor your messages accordingly. This targeted approach beats casting a wide net on social media and crossing your fingers, hoping your content connects.

The cherry on top? You can create an exclusive club for your email subscribers! Offering early-bird access to your new releases, special deals, or behind-the-scenes insights adds a sprinkle of exclusivity. This makes your subscribers feel cherished and valued, inspiring loyalty and encouraging them to spread the word about your work.

Now, let's clear something up: while building an email list might feel like trying to assemble a thousand-piece puzzle in the early stages, remember that every great journey starts with a single step.

Kickstart your email list building with a tantalising lead magnet - perhaps a sneak peek of your upcoming book or a handy guide. This freebie in exchange for their email address will pique your website visitors' interest and could nudge them to join your email community.

To boost your email sign-ups, consider adding a subscription form to your website and your email signature. You could also incentivize your social media followers to sign up by promising them access to exclusive content or special promotions.

Once you have a growing list of subscribers, it's a smart idea to segment them based on demographics, interests, and engagement. This allows you to craft personalised emails that will resonate more deeply with each reader segment.

Remember, gaining your audience's trust is key. Be upfront about what they can expect from your emails—how often they'll hear from you, what kind of content they'll receive—and make it easy for them to opt out if they wish. This transparency fosters a loyal and engaged email list, bolstering your brand awareness, generating leads, and boosting your sales.

Now, with all this talk of email lists, you might be wondering, "How do I get started?" Don't worry, I've got you covered! Let's explore some actionable steps you can take to build, nurture, and grow your email list effectively.

1. **Choose the Right Email Service Provider (ESP)**: There are numerous ESPs out there, each with its own features and benefits. Some popular choices for authors include Mailchimp, ConvertKit, and MailerLite. Consider your needs and budget when deciding on an ESP.

2. **Design an Irresistible Lead Magnet**: Think about what your readers would find valuable. It could be a free chapter from your latest book, a downloadable guide related to your genre, or even a bundle of your best writing tips. The goal is to offer something enticing enough that readers will willingly exchange their email address for it.

3. **Create a Landing Page for Your Lead Magnet**: This is a stand-alone webpage designed to promote your lead magnet and encourage sign-ups. The design should be clean, simple, and focused solely on getting visitors to enter their email.

4. **Promote Your Lead Magnet**: Share your lead magnet on social media, your blog, in guest posts, or even in your author bio at the end of your books. The more places you share it, the more opportunities you have to grow your list.

5. **Send a Warm Welcome Email**: Once someone signs up, greet them with a friendly welcome email. This should thank them for subscribing, deliver the promised lead magnet, and let them know what to expect from your future emails. A well-crafted welcome email sets the tone for your relationship with your new subscribers.

6. **Deliver Valuable Content Consistently**: Whether it's a monthly newsletter, writing tips, or updates about your work, make sure you're providing value to your subscribers. This not only keeps them engaged but also builds trust and strengthens your author-reader relationship.

7. **Encourage Sharing**: If your subscribers find your content valuable, chances are they know others who will, too. Include social share buttons and "Email to a Friend" options in your emails. You could even consider offering incentives for those who share your email with others, helping your list grow organically.

8. **Regularly Clean Your List**: Not all subscribers will stay engaged forever. Regularly cleaning your list—removing unengaged subscribers—keeps your list healthy and your open and click-through rates accurate.

Remember, building an email list takes time, but the return on investment can be tremendous. With each email sent, you're deepening your relationship with your readers, enhancing your brand's visibility, and building a community around your work. And that, dear author, is priceless.

Potential problems

I see you're diving into the nitty-gritty side of email list building—fantastic! It's true that, as rewarding as creating an email list can be, it comes with its own set of hurdles. But don't worry; just like a plot twist in a good book, these challenges only make the journey more interesting. Let's unpack some of these potential snags and how you can navigate them.

1. **Obtaining Consent**: Always, always, always get permission before adding someone to your list. Imagine someone adding you to a book club you didn't want to join—not cool, right? Consent is crucial to avoid spam complaints and unsubscribes, which can tarnish your reputation faster than a poorly proofread manuscript.

2. **Providing Value**: We all want our inboxes to be a treasure trove of useful content, not a graveyard of spammy messages. Make sure your emails offer value, whether it's in the form of enlightening articles, exclusive sneak peeks, or writing tips. Consistent, quality content will keep your subscribers tuned in and eagerly awaiting your next email.

3. **Staying Legally Compliant: Don't let GDPR-type data privacy regulations catch you off guard.** Ensuring your email marketing strategy is compliant can save you from some unpleasant (and potentially expensive) surprises. Your email service provider can often provide tools and resources to help you stay in line with these regulations.

4. **Segmentation and Personalization**: Not all of your readers are created equal; some might love your crime novels, while others are here for your poetry. Segmenting your list and sending targeted messages helps speak directly to your readers' interests, improving

engagement and reducing unsubscribes.

5. **Testing and Optimisation**: Even the best authors go through edits. Test your subject lines, content, and calls to action to see what works and what doesn't. Just a few tweaks here and there could significantly boost your open and click-through rates.

6. **Clear Calls to Action**: Your emails should have a purpose, whether it's sharing a new blog post, promoting a book, or announcing an event. A well-crafted call to action can be the difference between an email that gets results and one that gets ignored.

7. **Regular List Cleaning**: Just like your writing desk, your email list needs a regular clean-up. Inactive subscribers and bounced emails can make your list look messy and affect your deliverability rates. A clean list is a happy list, and a happy list leads to more successful campaigns!

Remember, like crafting a compelling narrative, building a successful email list requires time, effort, and a dash of creativity. You've got this!

What should your emails be about?

Wondering what to put in those emails you'll be sending out? Don't worry; it's like picking a theme for your next novel. As a self-publisher, you're already a content creation wizard! Think about it. Your books? Content. Printables? Content. Social media posts? Content. Everything you bring into existence can be the topic of your next email.

Here are a few ideas to keep those creative juices flowing:

1. **Teasers and Updates**: Give your subscribers a backstage pass to your creative process. Sharing sneak peeks into upcoming projects not only stirs up excitement, but also makes your readers feel like they're part of a secret club, getting the inside scoop before anyone else.

2. **New Releases**: The moment you publish a new book, printable, or other product, don't forget to share the thrilling news with your email list. It's like inviting them to a VIP book launch—they'll appreciate being in the know, and it might even lead to some immediate sales!

3. **Expert Tips and Insights**: You're not just an author; you're a guru in your niche. Share your wisdom with your audience. If you write self-help books, offer pearls of wisdom on personal growth. If you're a low-content book creator, provide guidance on making the most of planners or journals. Positioning yourself as an expert adds value to your emails, making them a resource your readers look forward to.

4. **Personal Stories**: Let your subscribers see the person behind the books. Share a heartfelt story or an experience that has shaped your work. This personal connection can turn casual readers into lifelong fans.

5. **Celebrate Success**: Just hit a sales milestone or published your tenth book? Pop the champagne and celebrate with your readers. Your victories are their victories too, and it shows them that their support plays a pivotal role in your journey.

6. **Exclusive Offers**: Treat your subscribers like the VIPs they are. Early access to your new releases, special promotions, or subscriber-only discounts can make them feel cherished and appreciated, increasing the chances of them turning into loyal customers.

7. **Engage and Interact**: Make your emails a two-way street. Ask for their opinions, throw in an intriguing question, or invite them to share their own stories. Encouraging dialogue fosters a sense of community, making your subscribers more invested in your work.

The secret ingredient for compelling emails? A cocktail of informative content, personal anecdotes, updates, and exclusive goodies, shaken well to suit your subscribers' tastes. This blend of content fosters an authentic connection with your audience and keeps them eagerly waiting for your next email.

Remember, the success of an email marketing strategy lies in finding the sweet spot between promotion and genuine engagement. With the right mix of updates, personal stories, exclusive content, and interactive elements, you'll keep your audience hooked and your author brand thriving.

How long should your emails be?

Wondering how long to make those emails you're planning to send out? It's a common question, and the answer is simpler than you might think. The ideal email length can depend on several factors, including the purpose of the email and its content. However, generally, less is often more when it comes to email length.

Your emails should be like a well-written novella: concise, captivating, and delivering a clear message. To make your emails digestible and reader-friendly, consider using headings, images, and bullet points to break up your text. Just like a well-structured book, this can make your emails visually pleasing and easy to scan through.

Also, keep in mind that many of your subscribers will likely read your emails on their mobile devices. So, making sure your emails are mobile-friendly is crucial.

As a general guide, consider keeping your emails within the 300–500 word range. Of course, this isn't set in stone and can vary based on your content and audience. What's important is keeping your message succinct and to the point.

And remember, there's always room for a bit of experimentation. Don't hesitate to try out different lengths and structures for your emails. Testing is a great way to discover what engages your audience the most.

To sum it up, while there isn't a one-size-fits-all length for emails, shorter and more focused emails often resonate best with readers. Keep your content clear, make it scannable, ensure it's mobile-friendly, and don't forget to enjoy the process of experimenting.

How often should you email your list?

Wondering about the frequency of sending emails to your list? It's a balance between delivering valuable and engaging content to your subscribers without overwhelming or turning them off.

A good place to start might be to email your list once a week. But this isn't a one-size-fits-all solution. Your email frequency can depend on several factors, such as your audience and the nature of the content you're sending. If you're running an online store with frequent product launches, you might find it beneficial to send emails more often. If you're a blogger who posts weekly, a weekly email might suit your rhythm.

The nature of your content also plays a key role. If you're sending promotional emails, you might want to limit those to one or two a month. On the other hand, educational content can typically be shared more frequently without annoying your audience.

Remember, your subscribers are unique individuals with their own preferences. Consider giving them the option to decide how frequently they want to hear from you. This way, some might opt to stay more connected, while others will appreciate fewer, yet more impactful, emails.

Be mindful of the email frequency, though. Too many emails can lead to unsubscribes and dwindling engagement. Conversely, too few emails might make your list seem inactive and allow your subscribers to forget about you.

As an author, the frequency of your emails might also depend on:

- Educational content: If you're sharing writing tips, industry updates, or author Q&As, a weekly email might be perfectly fine.

- Book Club or Reading Group Opportunities: If you're providing these opportunities, you might need to send emails more often to fuel participation and engagement.

So there's no hard-and-fast rule. Your ideal email frequency will depend on several factors, such as your content type, business stage, and subscribers' preferences. The main goal should always be to offer valuable content without being a nuisance.

In my journey, sending emails once a week worked well, but the important thing is to find the frequency that fits you and your audience like a glove. Good luck finding your perfect balance!

Make sure to back up your list weekly!

Don't forget to give your email list the weekly TLC (Tender Loving Care) it needs – by backing it up!

Why should you do this, you ask? Here are a few compelling reasons:

1. **Safeguard against data loss:** It's like an insurance policy for your email list! Regular backups can shield your precious data from unforeseen accidents like data deletion, hardware glitches, or software hiccups. So, backing up your list weekly drastically reduces the risk of losing your valuable subscriber data.

2. **Ensure business continuity:** Your email list is your business's lifeblood. If technical issues or data loss strike, having a recent backup can help you maintain seamless communication with your subscribers and promote your offerings without skipping a beat.

3. **Guard against cyber threats:** In today's digital age, cyber threats like hacking or ransomware are real and menacing. Regular backups act like a security fortress, enabling you to restore your list to

a secure state if it ever gets compromised.

4. **Stay compliant with data protection regulations:** Regularly backing up your email list keeps you equipped with a secure and updated record of your subscribers' information, which is crucial for compliance with data protection regulations like GDPR.

Now, how can you back up your email list weekly? Here are some handy methods:

- **Export and save:** Most email marketing platforms let you export your email list as a CSV or Excel file. Just save this file on your computer and make additional copies on external hard drives or USB drives for that extra layer of security.

- **Cloud-based backup:** Leverage cloud storage services like Google Drive, Dropbox, or OneDrive to store a copy of your email list. These services work like magic, syncing your data across devices to ensure you always have an up-to-date backup.

- **Backup software:** You might want to consider investing in back-up software that automates the whole process of backing up your email list and other vital business data.

- **Third-party email list backup service:** There are services that specialise in backing up email lists, offering additional features like encryption, versioning, and recovery options.

- **Mix and match:** Combine the above methods for the best protection. For instance, export and save your email list on your computer while also storing a copy on a cloud-based backup service.

Remember, backing up your email list weekly is key to keeping your data safe and ensuring business continuity. Pick the backup method that suits your needs best and make it a part of your weekly routine. After all, your email list is the crown jewel of your publishing business! So, it's only wise to protect it and keep it secure.

What you should and shouldn't do with your list

Navigating the world of email lists involves striking a delicate balance between what you should and shouldn't do. Here's a map to guide you:

Do's:

1. **Strike a balance with offers:** Offering freebies can be a magnet for new subscribers, but tread carefully. If you offer too much for free, you might discourage future purchases.

2. **Stay in touch:** Don't let your absence make your subscribers forget about you. Keep in touch even if you don't have a new product or service to promote.

3. **Prioritise privacy with a PO Box:** Privacy and security come first. Include a physical postal address in your emails for trust-building and legal compliance. But for your safety, opt for a PO Box instead. Services like UK Postbox or Convertkit can help with this.

4. **Deliver value:** Make your emails worthwhile for your subscribers. Ditch the constant sales pitches and provide information or entertainment instead. Be mindful of the frequency of your sales offers and link sharing.

5. **Adopt a positive and motivational tone:** Positivity breeds trust and strengthens relationships. Don't forget to thank your subscribers for their engagement and support.

Don'ts:

1. **Don't spam your subscribers:** Avoid constant sales pitches and spam. Give them a breather from being sold to.

When it comes to talking to your email list, remember that you're interacting with real people with unique needs and concerns. To effectively communicate with them:

- **Tell stories:** Stories draw people in and create emotional connections. Whether you share personal experiences or case studies, stories can make your brand more relatable.

- **Address their pain points:** Offering solutions to their problems can increase engagement with your content. Understand their concerns and offer valuable and actionable insights.

- **Maintain your brand voice:** Consistency in your tone and personality makes your brand easily recognisable and more trustworthy.

- **Be personal and conversational:** Skip formal language or jargon; opt for a friendly and approachable tone. This can enhance trust and encourage engagement.

- **Say 'thank you':** Show your gratitude for their support and engagement. This strengthens the bond with your subscribers and cultivates loyalty.

Remember, communicating with your subscribers isn't a one-size-fits-all approach; it's an art that requires understanding their needs and interests. So, tell engaging stories, offer solutions, maintain your brand voice, use friendly language, and express gratitude to create emails that resonate with your subscribers and build lasting relationships.

Should you worry about unsubscribers?

Should you sweat over unsubscribers? They are not your people, after all!

When someone opts out of your email list, it may simply indicate that they aren't the right fit for your business. There are myriad reasons why someone might unsubscribe: accidental sign-up, changing interests, or finding a better fit elsewhere.

Take these unsubscribes in stride rather than personally. Shift your attention towards the engagement and conversions of your remaining subscribers. These are the folks who are genuinely interested in your business and likely to engage and transact.

Use unsubscribes as learning opportunities to refine your email strategy. A detailed analysis of unsubscribes can reveal subscribers' preferences, allowing you to tailor your emails to their needs, enhance engagement, and boost conversions. For instance, by identifying emails with high unsubscribe rates, you can pinpoint issues: was the subject line unappealing or was the content off-target?

Understand that unsubscribes are an integral part of email marketing. Instead of letting them dishearten you, view them as triggers for betterment. Make the unsubscribe process straightforward to reduce spam complaints and preserve your business reputation.

Remember, housing inactive subscribers can drain your resources. These are subscribers who have stopped opening or interacting with your emails over time. Regularly cleaning and pruning your email list to weed out such inactive subscribers can result in cost savings and lets you focus on engaging the truly interested ones.

Many email marketing platforms charge based on subscriber count, so a smaller but highly engaged list can help cut costs. By regularly culling your email list, you can focus on the subscribers who are genuinely invested in your business, allowing you to optimise your engagement and marketing resources.

Find your email style!

Do you ever find yourself engrossed in reading an email, even if the subject isn't particularly fascinating to you? That's the magic some email marketers weave with their engaging and enjoyable writing style. Finding your distinct email style is crucial for nurturing robust, lasting bonds with your subscribers. It's all about unearthing the voice and tone that best mirror your brand and resonate with your audience.

Here's a handy tip: scrutinise the emails you love reading. What draws you to them? The tone, the language, the structure? Observing the characteristics you find appealing can give you valuable insights into the style you might want to mirror in your own emails.

You could also experiment with various tones and formats. Try out emails with a formal tone, then switch to a casual one and compare the results. Test out different formats as well, such as shorter versus longer emails or ones with more or fewer visuals. These experiments can help you identify what resonates best with your audience and your business.

Don't forget: your email style should be a mirror reflection of your brand's persona. Whether your brand voice is formal or informal, consistency is key to building trust and recognition with your subscribers.

And finally, be bold enough to ask your subscribers for feedback. Ask them what they think of your emails – what they like or dislike, what they wish to see more of. Such direct feedback can help you understand what truly resonates with your audience and enable you to fine-tune your email style accordingly.

In a nutshell, discovering your email style involves experimentation and understanding what suits your business and audience best. It's all about identifying the tone and voice that best embody your brand, resonate with your audience, and consistently reflect your brand persona. Be open to experimentation, feedback, and ongoing testing to refine the perfect email style for your business.

Your email style should align with your audience's preferences and the message you aim to convey. It's equally crucial to continually test and experiment to perfect your email style. Here are some exercises that might help you sculpt your email style:

Casual and conversational:

- Craft a conversation between you and a friend discussing a topic related to your business. Use this chat as inspiration for the tone and language of your emails.

- Compile a list of words and phrases you'd typically use in a friendly chat and infuse these into your emails.

- Write a letter to a friend introducing your business and offerings. Use this letter as a springboard for your welcome email.

Educational and informative:

- Research common questions or hurdles your target audience faces and make a list. Use this as a catalyst for crafting useful and informative emails addressing these pain points.

- Create an email series packed with valuable resources and information, including tips, tutorials, or recommended readings.

- Draft an email educating subscribers on something new about your industry or business.

Storytelling:

- Sketch a storyboard for a brand story you want to tell through your emails, outlining the characters, setting, and plot.

- Write an email narrating a personal story about the inception of your business or the development of a product or service.

- Share a case study showcasing how your business helped a customer overcome a problem.

Sales and promotions:

- List your products and services and brainstorm various ways to promote them via email.

- Draft an email promoting a sale or special offer.

- Inject a sense of urgency into your email by spotlighting a limited-time offer or a product that's quickly running out of stock.

Newsletters:

- Compile a list of recent updates in your business to share with your subscribers.

- Write a newsletter providing a roundup of the latest happenings in your business, including new products, services, and events

Remember, developing your email style isn't a one-time event but a continuous process of learning and evolving. Try out these exercises, and you'll likely discover not only what resonates best with your audience but also what truly represents your brand and feels most authentic to you. Your unique email style could be a blend of various elements, and that's perfectly fine.

Once you've found your email style, stick to it. Consistency will help your subscribers instantly recognise your brand's emails. It might feel a bit daunting at first, but with time, you'll see that your email style becomes a natural extension of your brand.

In the end, remember to be patient with yourself. You don't need to have it all figured out at once. Just like building a brand, finding your style takes time. But once you've found it, it will feel like the last piece of a puzzle, making your brand image complete.

How to grow your list

Let's talk about growing your email list. Have you heard of a lead magnet? If not, let me introduce you to your new best friend in the world of email marketing. Picture this: it's a tantalising offer, so tempting that your potential customers happily trade their email addresses for it. Neat, right?

Lead magnets can be your golden ticket to list growth. But it's not just about collecting email addresses. Lead magnets also give you the chance to share valuable content that positions you as the whiz you are in your industry. It's like giving your potential customers a sneak peek into the amazing value you can provide.

Not sure how to create your lead magnet? Don't worry, I've got you covered!

First, nurture your leads. Just like a house plant, your list needs regular care. Keep your subscribers engaged with helpful, interesting content that connects with them on a deeper level.

Now, if you're scratching your head over what your freebie could be, let's brainstorm together! Depending on what kind of writer you are, here are a few ideas:

For the fiction writers among us:

- Offer a free e-book of your latest novel's captivating first chapter.

- Share a short story or novella that only your email subscribers can get their hands on.

- Give away a writing guide loaded with your personal tips for creating gripping characters and storylines.

And for my non-fiction writer friends:

- A sneak peek into your latest book with a free e-book or PDF of the introduction or a chapter.

- Share a how-to guide or a checklist about a topic you're an expert in.

- Provide a free video course that takes viewers behind the scenes of your writing or research process.

If you're a low-content book creator:

- A printable or digital worksheet, planner, or journal page to get started.

- An e-book or PDF filled with your best advice on using your books.

- If you make colouring books, offer free colouring pages related to your niche.

Remember, your lead magnet should be something your audience will find valuable, and it should showcase your expertise. Whether it's a guide, an e-book, a video course, a checklist, or a worksheet, the goal is to offer something they'd be excited to exchange their contact information for. And, most importantly, your lead magnet should feel like a warm hug from you to your audience, showcasing all the wonderful things you can do for them. So go ahead, grow your email list, and make some amazing connections along the way!

Delivering your Lead Magnet

So, you've come up with a fantastic idea for a lead magnet. Great! But how do you get it to your customers? Don't fret! I've got a step-by-step guide to help you deliver that shiny lead magnet right into your customers' inboxes.

1. **Create Your Lead Magnet**: First things first, it's time to bring your lead magnet to life. Whether it's an engaging e-book, a handy checklist, or an insightful webinar, make sure it's something that your audience will find valuable and enticing enough to join your email list.

2. **Set Up a Landing Page**: Next, you'll need a home for your lead magnet—a landing page! Here, your visitors can learn all about the awesome content you're offering. Make it enticing with an attention-grabbing headline, a quick rundown of what they'll get, and a bright, hard-to-miss call-to-action (CTA) button to sign up.

3. **Pick Your Email Marketing Platform**: Platforms like Mailchimp, ConvertKit, or MailerLite are perfect for managing your email list and delivering your lead magnet. They often come with in-built tools for creating landing pages and delivering lead magnets, which is super handy.

4. **Set Up the Delivery Process**: Within your chosen platform, you'll set up an automatic email sequence that kicks into gear the moment someone signs up. The first email will contain the link to your lead magnet, a warm welcome message, and a friendly introduction to your brand.

5. **Promote Your Lead Magnet**: Now, it's time to shout from the rooftops about your lead magnet. Share the link on your website, social media, blog posts, or anywhere you engage with your audience. Spice up your promotions with appealing visuals and catchy CTAs to draw people in.

6. **Monitor and Optimise:** Keep an eye on how your lead magnet campaign is doing. Are people signing up? Are they opening your emails? Use the analytics tools from your email marketing platform to track these metrics and tweak your strategies based on what's working and what's not.

7. **Follow Up**: After your lead magnet is sent, don't forget to check in. Send a friendly automated email to ensure they received the lead magnet and ask if they have any questions or feedback.

And that's it! By following these steps, you'll not only deliver your lead magnet smoothly but also set the stage for a great relationship with your new subscribers. Happy emailing!

Not so fictional case study

Let's dive into a real-world story of email list success. To protect privacy, I've switched up the names, but the journey and the triumph are as real as they get.

Let's put a spotlight on Jane, a dynamite low-content book creator who is making waves with her thoughtfully designed journals and planners. But here's the catch: Jane didn't always have a throng of email subscribers hanging onto her every word. She started as a small fry with big dreams of growing her email list and elevating her business. Spoiler alert: She totally nailed it!

Jane kicked off her journey by playing detective. She wanted to know her audience, and so she discovered that journal enthusiasts and self-improvement buffs were her kind of people. With her audience in mind, she whipped up an irresistible lead magnet—a free printable journal spread. Then she built a landing page and started broadcasting the good news about her lead magnet across her website and social media channels. And voila! Her target audience flocked to her like kids to an ice cream truck.

With her email list getting bigger and better, Jane made it a point to keep her subscribers in the loop about her newest offerings. But she went one step further—she sprinkled some exclusivity by giving her email subscribers special discounts and promotions. It was like being in a VIP club!

Jane didn't stop there. She rolled out a referral programme where her subscribers could score a discount on their next purchase if they referred friends and family. This brilliant move not only expanded her email list but also fostered a sense of community among her customers.

Guess what happened next? Jane saw her sales and revenue hit new highs. She had a band of loyal customers who loved her products and eagerly shared her business with their friends and family. Growing her email list turned out to be a game-changing move for Jane's low-content book business.

Jane's story isn't just about a low-content book creator. It's about a determined woman who dreamed big, took the right steps, and achieved her goals. By understanding her audience, crafting a compelling lead magnet, promoting it effectively, and nurturing her email list, she boosted her sales and revenue and built a community of devoted customers. Her referral programme was the cherry on top, further growing her list and strengthening her community. Here's to Jane, a shining example of how building and nurturing an email list can propel a business to new heights!

And last but not least...

There are a few more tidbits that might be helpful for you to consider when creating your email list.

1. **Double Opt-In:** Though we've talked a lot about the mechanics of growing your email list, it's essential not to overlook the quality of your subscribers. Implementing a double opt-in process, where subscribers have to confirm their email address after signing up, can be a great way to ensure you're building a list of people who are genuinely interested in your content. It might seem like an extra step, but it helps sift out those who might have signed up impulsively or by mistake.

2. **Segmentation and Personalization:** Once you've got a burgeoning list, it's a great idea to start segmenting it. Segmentation simply means dividing your email list into smaller groups based on certain criteria. It could be anything from the type of lead magnet they signed up for, their location, or even their activity level. Once you've got your list segmented, you can start personalising your emails, which can significantly increase engagement. It's like having a chat with an old friend; if they feel you 'get them', they're more likely to stay engaged.

3. **Test, Test, Test:** Never underestimate the power of A/B testing! Try out different subject lines, email formats, sending times, and even CTA placements. Analysing the results will give you a deeper understanding of what resonates with your audience and can significantly boost your open and click-through rates.

4. **Email List Hygiene:** It may sound a bit odd, but keeping your list 'clean' is a great way to maintain high engagement rates and sender reputation. Regularly removing inactive subscribers—those who never open your emails or have outdated email addresses—can actually increase the overall performance of your email list. It's like tending a garden—sometimes you need to pull out the weeds to let the other plants thrive!

5. **Providing Value Consistently:** Finally, always remember that your emails should provide value. Whether it's useful tips, interesting stories, or exclusive deals, make sure every email you send adds something to your subscriber's day. People are quick to unsubscribe from lists that don't meet their expectations, so focus on creating high-quality content that your readers will look forward to!

I hope these additional insights make your email list journey even more successful. Remember, building a fantastic email list isn't a one-time event; it's a continuous process of learning, adapting, and growing. So, here's to your thriving email list, reaching more people, and making your mark in your chosen field!

"A successful website is built with persistence, nurtured with creativity, and sustained by the connections it creates."

Social Media

Connecting and Engaging

How can social media help build your brand?

Let's talk about the world of social media. Now, I know what you might be thinking: "Social media? That's a full-time job!" You're not entirely wrong; social media can be a bit of a beast. But when tamed correctly, it can do wonders for your author brand.

There are so many social media platforms out there that it might seem overwhelming. The key is to find the ones that work best for you. Not all platforms are created equal, and not all of them will serve your specific needs as an author or a low-content book creator.

Platforms like Facebook, Twitter, and Instagram are great for both authors and publishers because of their wide user base and flexibility in content sharing. Here, you can share book snippets, behind-the-scenes peeks, and even interact with your readers.

For low-content book creators, visual platforms like Pinterest or Instagram can be ideal as they allow you to showcase the aesthetic appeal of your books, templates, or designs. LinkedIn, on the other hand, might be less relevant unless you're writing or publishing in a professional or business niche.

Remember, you don't have to be on all platforms. Choose one or two that align with your target audience and your comfort zone. After all, the best platform is the one where you can consistently engage with your readers and potential customers.

We'll delve more into what to post on these platforms later. But for now, take some time to explore these platforms and see which ones resonate with you and your brand.

As an author, you might be wondering which social media platforms will give you the best results in terms of reaching your target audience and promoting your work. The truth is, there's no one-size-fits-all answer, as the ideal platform for you will depend on your goals, target audience, and personal preferences. Let's explore some popular social media platforms, including LinkedIn and YouTube, and discuss their benefits for authors. Armed with this information, you can make an informed decision about which platforms will work best for your author brand.

Facebook: A Platform for Building Communities

Facebook is a great platform for authors looking to build a community around their work. With its wide user base and various features such as Facebook Pages, Groups, and Events, you can create a dedicated space for your readers to interact, share updates, and promote your book launches and signings. Plus, Facebook's advertising options can help you reach a larger audience with targeted promotions.

If you enjoy fostering connections with your readers and hosting discussions, Facebook might be the perfect platform for your author brand.

Instagram: A Visual Storytelling Haven

Instagram is a visually driven platform that offers a unique opportunity for authors to share their stories through images, short videos, and interactive stories. If you have a knack for creating visually appealing content such as book covers, aesthetic images, and behind-the-scenes glimpses of your writing process, Instagram could be the platform for you.

Additionally, Instagram's hashtag system can help you connect with readers interested in your genre and build a loyal following of book lovers.

Twitter: Quick Updates and Real-Time Engagement

Twitter's fast-paced, real-time environment is ideal for authors who enjoy sharing quick updates, engaging in conversations, and connecting with other writers and influencers in their genre. With its 280-character limit, Twitter forces you to be concise and creative with your words—a challenge that many authors find enjoyable.

Participating in Twitter's popular writing-related hashtags and events like #WritingCommunity and #PitMad can help you expand your network and discover new opportunities in the publishing world.

LinkedIn: Networking with Industry Professionals

LinkedIn is a professional networking platform that allows you to connect with other authors, publishers, and industry professionals. By creating an author profile, you can showcase your work, share updates, and engage with relevant groups to expand your network and stay informed about industry trends.

If you're looking to build connections within the publishing world and establish yourself as a professional author, LinkedIn is an excellent platform to consider.

YouTube: Share Your Story Through Video

YouTube is a video-sharing platform that offers authors a unique opportunity to connect with their audience through engaging video content. By creating a YouTube channel, you can share book trailers, author interviews, writing tips, and behind-the-scenes glimpses of your writing process.

If you're comfortable in front of the camera and enjoy creating video content, YouTube can be a powerful tool to showcase your personality and connect with your audience on a deeper level.

Goodreads: The Social Network for Book Lovers

Goodreads is a social network dedicated to book lovers, making it an ideal platform for authors to connect with their target audience. By creating an author profile, you can showcase your work, interact with readers, and participate in the Goodreads community through book clubs, giveaways, and Q&A sessions.

While not a traditional social media platform, Goodreads allows you to focus solely on your writing and connect with readers who are genuinely interested in your genre.

Pinterest: A Visual Discovery Tool for Inspiration and Promotion

Pinterest is a visual search engine and discovery tool where users create and share boards of images related to specific topics, making it a great platform for sharing inspiration and promoting your work. As an author, you can create boards featuring your book covers, character inspirations, and settings from your novels, allowing readers to get a better sense of your creative vision. Additionally, Pinterest is an excellent platform for sharing blog posts, articles, and writing tips that can drive traffic back to your author website.

If you enjoy curating visually appealing content and want to give your readers a unique glimpse into your creative process, Pinterest could be a fantastic choice.

As you can see, each social media platform offers unique benefits for authors. The key to success is to choose platforms that align with your goals, strengths, and target audience. You don't have to be present on every platform; instead, focus on the ones that resonate with you and your readers.

Experiment with different platforms and analyse your engagement and growth to determine which ones work best for your author brand. By leveraging the power of social media, you can build a strong online presence and connect with readers in a way that feels authentic and enjoyable.

Please note that the social media landscape is constantly evolving, with platforms frequently updating their features, algorithms, and policies. While the information presented here is accurate and relevant at the time of writing, it's essential to stay informed about any changes that may impact your author branding strategy. To keep up with the latest trends and best practises, consider following industry news, joining author communities, and regularly reviewing the guidelines and recommendations provided by each platform. Staying adaptable and flexible in your approach will ensure that your social media presence remains effective and engaging, even as the digital world continues to change.

Wow, that's a lot of social media platforms. Which ones should you choose for your brand?

Picking the Right Dance Partners: Choosing Your Social Media Platforms

Phew! Who knew there were so many social media platforms out there? It's like walking into a party with a sea of faces and wondering where on earth to start. Should you befriend everyone in the room or just focus on a few people? Well, let's figure this out together.

Now, I know it's tempting to sign up for every social media platform that pops up on your radar. It's like being at a buffet and wanting to try everything. But if we overfill our plates, we might not be able to savour each dish, right? And, let's be honest, we could end up with a social media stomachache! So, rather than spreading yourself too thin, let's aim for one or two platforms that suit you and your audience, like a well-tailored book cover.

Remember, consistency and engagement are the secret ingredients in our social media recipe. By focusing on just a couple of platforms, you can pour your heart into creating meaningful content and forging genuine connections with your audience. If you try to be everywhere at once, you might end up sacrificing content quality and that precious reader connection.

"But how do I choose my platforms?" I hear you asking. Well, it's like picking the perfect book club for your novel. First, think about who your readers are, their likes, and how they hang out online. If your audience is young adults, you might strike gold with Instagram over LinkedIn or Facebook.

Then consider your strengths and preferences. It's like choosing between writing a mystery novel or a romance book—go with what you enjoy and are good at. If you love sharing your story through videos, YouTube might be your jam. If you love sharing short updates and enjoying conversations, Twitter could be your cosy nook.

Remember, there's no one-size-fits-all answer here. It's all about picking the platforms that serve both your audience and your unique strengths. When you invest your time and energy into these select few, you're likely to build a strong, authentic bond with your readers and boost your author brand.

Time for a pro tip!

Social media schedulers can be a lifesaver, helping you keep a consistent presence on your chosen platforms without running yourself ragged. Think of them like your personal social media butler, planning, creating, and scheduling your content in advance and making sure it's served at the right time to your audience. It's like hosting a perfectly timed and catered party with minimal stress.

These schedulers help streamline your content creation process, and many come with built-in analytics tools that act like a popularity meter, showing you which posts are winning hearts. Popular options include Buffer, Hootsuite, and Later. I personally use Later and find it as easy as pie to use. It adjusts your post size for each platform, so no more awkwardly cropped images! Canva also has a scheduler, although it might be a little more basic, but hey, it could be a great start.

In the world of social media, schedulers can be your secret weapon. They help you focus more on writing and connecting with your audience while still maintaining a strong and consistent online presence.

Alright, deep breath; you're doing great! Ready to dive into the next exciting chapter: What to Post on Social Media? Let's do it!

The Art of Posting: Content Ideas for Authors and Low-Content Book Creators

Now that we've got our social media platforms sorted out, let's tackle the next beast: what to post. This part is where most of us get stuck, isn't it? We've all had that moment where we stare at the screen, fingers hovering over the keyboard, wondering what on earth to share.

First and foremost, remember that social media is about being social! It's not just a broadcasting platform. It's a place to start conversations, engage with readers, and build a community. That's why it's essential to not just talk about your books or products all the time. Yes, you're there to promote your work, but it's also about adding value, connecting, and entertaining.

As an author, you could share:

1. Quotes from your books

2. Updates on your writing progress

3. Behind-the-scenes peeks into your writing life

4. Book recommendations

5. Q&A sessions about your writing process or characters

For low-content book creators, your posts could be:

1. Sneak peeks of your upcoming books

2. Templates or worksheets that tie into your low-content books

3. Tips and advice on how to use your products

4. User testimonials or photos of your products in use

5. Q&A sessions about your creation process or upcoming projects

Now, remember the golden rule of social media: consistency. Whether you post once a day or once a week, find a schedule that works for you and stick with it. Consistency is key to keeping your audience engaged and growing your following.

The beauty of social media is the chance to experiment. Don't be afraid to try out different kinds of posts and see what your audience responds to best. And most importantly, have fun with it! Your passion and enthusiasm will shine through your posts, attracting those who resonate with your work.

We've talked about what to post, now let's talk about how often and when to post on social media.

Nailing the Posting Rhythm: When and How Often to Post

Hello there! How's the social media adventure treating you? If you're feeling a bit lost about how often and when to post, don't worry; we've all been there. The world of social media can be a little overwhelming at first. But remember, we're in this together, and I'm here to guide you through it.

First off, there's no 'one-size-fits-all' solution when it comes to posting frequency. It's like picking out the perfect outfit—what works wonderfully for one person might not work for another. It depends on your goals, who you're trying to reach, and which platforms you're using. But don't fret; I have some handy guidelines to help you find your groove:

Posting Frequency: Consistency is your new best friend. Whether you're the 'post everyday' type or more of a 'few times a week' person, find a rhythm that suits you and stick to it. You're building a relationship with your audience here. You wouldn't want your friends to randomly disappear on you, right? Personally, I found that posting once a day keeps my audience engaged and lets them know I'm here, doing my thing.

Content Variety: Shake things up! Keep your audience on their toes with a mix of different content. Try some promotional posts about your book releases or events, educational posts with tips or insights, inspiring quotes or stories, engaging questions or polls, and a sprinkle of personal updates or behind-the-scenes peeks.

Platform-Specific Content: Let's not wear a cocktail dress to a beach party, shall we? Tailor your content to match the platform you're on. Instagram loves a good photo, so give them dazzling book covers or intriguing behind-the-scenes shots. Twitter, on the other hand, thrives on short updates and engaging conversations, while Facebook gives you room to stretch out with longer posts, events, and groups.

Timing: Timing, like comedy, is everything. Post when your audience is most likely to be online and ready to engage. Each platform has analytics tools to help you find out when your audience is most active. It's like throwing a party—you want to make sure your guests can actually attend, right?

Analyse and Adjust: Keep a close eye on how your posts are doing. Check the likes, comments, and shares, and watch your follower count. If a certain type of post gets a lot of love, consider giving your audience more of what they like. Remember, it's all about engaging your audience.

So, there you have it! The magic formula for social media success is consistency, engagement, and adaptability. Feel free to experiment, find out what works best for you and your brand, and remember—have fun with it! In the end, it's all about connecting with your audience and sharing the journey with them.

Phew! That was quite a bit. Ready to dive into the next part? We're just getting warmed up!

The Art of Social Listening and Community Engagement

Just when you thought we'd covered all the social media bases, here's another surprise: social listening and community engagement. Now, don't get frazzled; these might sound like tech jargon, but they're really just a fancy way of saying 'paying attention' and 'being sociable'.

Imagine you're at a book club meeting, and you're discussing a novel. It's not just about voicing your opinion, right? You listen to what others have to say, respond to their points, and build upon the discussion. That's precisely what social listening and community engagement are about.

Social listening is like being a detective. It's about paying attention to what your audience (and even your competitors) are saying online. Are they raving about a particular book genre? Are they sharing tips for overcoming writer's block? Observing these conversations gives you valuable insights into what your audience is interested in and what content might resonate with them.

Next comes community engagement, and this is the heart of social media. It's all about being more than a voice broadcasting content. You're part of a community! So, take part in the conversation, respond to comments, thank people for their shares, and don't shy away from joining discussions that interest you. This kind of engagement shows your audience that you're not just an author but a person they can connect with.

Also, let's not forget about handling criticism. We all know how it feels to get a negative review or comment. It's like someone saying they don't like your favourite book. Ouch! But remember, it's important to handle criticism gracefully online. Thank them for their feedback, take on board what's constructive, and always stay professional.

And finally, have fun! Social media isn't just about promoting your work; it's also a space to let your personality shine through. Share your writing journey, celebrate your milestones, and don't be afraid to share your non-writing passions too. Who knows, your love for gardening or vintage postcards might resonate with your readers!

So there you go—the world of social media isn't as daunting as it first seems, right? It's a playground for you to connect, engage, learn, and grow as an author. So, take a deep breath, dive in, and let your author brand flourish!

"Remember, you're not just building a following on social media; you're building a community. Be genuine, be consistent, and watch your audience grow."

Once Upon A Social Media Post

Discovering the Power of Branding Through a Fictional Journey

Let's take a break from the theory and embark on a make-believe journey. No, we're not diving into the latest fantasy novel; instead, we're exploring the realm of branding through a fictional case study. I promise you, it's just as exciting!

See, the beauty of a fictional case study is that it lets our imagination run wild, exploring different branding strategies without the fear of making real-life blunders. It's a bit like playing a business simulation game, but with more creativity and a dash of fun.

Our imaginary journey could reveal the pros and cons of various strategies, helping you figure out what might be the secret sauce for your own brand. It's like a mental dress rehearsal for your real-world branding strategy, letting you test out scenarios and foresee potential outcomes.

Plus, a fictional case study makes complex ideas easier to grasp. It's a story-telling method that provides an engaging and relatable way to remember concepts and strategies. And, of course, it highlights the power of social media to shape a brand's success.

Now, without further ado, allow me to introduce our fictional friend, Jane Smith, the imaginative mastermind behind a flourishing publishing business.

Jane is a whiz at creating low-content books, from handy journals and planners to delightful colouring books. Initially, she sold her creations on Amazon and Etsy. Yet Jane had a hunch that her brand could soar higher with a strong social media presence. So she embarked on her Instagram journey.

Her Instagram business page soon became a vibrant showcase of her products, sprinkled with glimpses of her creative process and useful tips for her followers. Jane didn't stop at posting; she made sure to interact with other creators in her niche, sharing their posts and dropping friendly comments. Voila! Relationships blossomed, and her follower count bloomed.

Embracing Instagram's shoppable posts feature, Jane tagged her products, allowing followers to shop right from the app—a breeze for her busy customers and an effortless way to boost her sales.

Jane didn't put all her eggs in the Instagram basket, though. She hopped onto Pinterest, creating dedicated boards for each product line. She strategically pinned images, making sure to sprinkle relevant keywords to draw in new customers searching for products like hers.

She further cemented her brand by hosting exciting giveaways and contests. These not only expanded her follower base but fostered an engaged community of customers who were more likely to hit the 'buy now' button and recommend her products to others.

Customer testimonials and reviews are regularly featured on Jane's channels, fortifying the trust and credibility of her brand. The result? An expanded following, increased sales, and soaring brand awareness. Her business took flight, and Jane Smith became a celebrated name in the low-content book world.

The journey of our make-believe friend, Jane, reveals the magic that a well-strategised social media plan can weave for your brand. From leveraging shoppable posts and Pinterest to hosting contests, every decision contributed to building her loyal customer base and thriving business.

This little peek into Jane's story serves as a reminder that social media, coupled with a robust branding strategy, can transform your business into a flourishing empire. And remember, with a dash of creativity, branding can be more fun than daunting! So, let's draw inspiration from Jane's journey and get ready to map out your own path to branding success.

"The journey of a thousand engaged subscribers begins with a single email. Start building your list today and watch the magic unfold!"

Chapter Nine

Let's Recap

Your 4 Step Checklist

We've travelled quite a bit through the world of branding for self-publishers, haven't we? I hope you've found it enlightening and empowering so far, even though I know it can be a lot to take in. Breathe in, breathe out. It's all good.

Remember, this isn't a race, but a journey of learning and discovery. It's about understanding the key elements that make up your author brand and how you can bring them all together to communicate effectively with your audience. If you're feeling a bit overwhelmed, that's perfectly okay. You're not alone. This is a big topic, and it's completely normal to feel this way.

To help you navigate this world of branding a little more smoothly, I've broken down the most important tasks or elements for your brand into four essential steps. Think of these as your roadmap, your guiding star, or your check-off list in the great adventure of building your author brand.

These steps are designed to break down the most critical tasks of branding into manageable chunks. So you can not only understand them but also make them work for you. Remember, you're not expected to master everything at once. Take your time with each step, implement them at your own pace, and always keep your unique vision as an author in mind.

By focusing on these four key areas, you'll have a solid foundation for your brand. A brand that truly reflects you, resonates with your target audience, and helps your books shine in the world of self-publishing. And you can apply everything you have learned so far. So, let's dive in and explore these four essential steps to building your author brand!

1: Building Your Author Website

A professional, easy-to-navigate author website is the cornerstone of your online author brand. It's where readers can learn more about you, your books, and any upcoming events or releases. Moreover, it's a platform you control entirely, unlike social media channels, where algorithms can affect your visibility.

Start by purchasing a domain name that ideally incorporates your author name or brand. Select a reliable website host, choose a clean and easy-to-navigate design, and fill it with engaging content. The content should include an about page, a book list with links to purchase them, a contact form, and a blog if you plan to maintain one. Remember, the website should reflect your brand's tone and style.

Exercise: Outline the structure of your website. What pages will it have? What kind of content will you share? What visuals represent your brand?

2: Setting Up an Amazon Author Central Account

Next on the list is setting up your Amazon Author Central account. This is your command centre on Amazon. You can manage your presence, track your book sales, and interact with your readers here. Your author profile is the perfect place to showcase your professional author photos, your bio, and a link to your website.

Exercise: Write a compelling author bio for your Amazon Author Central account. It should introduce you, highlight your writing credentials, and invite readers to engage with your brand further.

3: Building and Maintaining Your Email List

Building an email list is one of the most effective ways to maintain direct contact with your readers. By offering incentives like free chapters, behind-the-scenes access, or newsletters with exclusive content, you can encourage visitors to your website to subscribe to your email list.

Exercise: Come up with an enticing incentive to encourage visitors to subscribe to your email list. Outline the content of your first newsletter.

4. Social Media Accounts:

Social media offers you the opportunity to connect with your audience on a more personal level. Choose platforms where your target audience spends time – this could be Twitter, Facebook, Instagram, LinkedIn, or others. Be consistent in your posting, share valuable content, and engage with your followers.

Exercise: Create a social media strategy. Choose your platforms, outline the types of content you'll share, and schedule your posts.

Now that we've walked through the initial four steps—building your author website, setting up your Amazon Author Central account, creating and maintaining your email list, and establishing your social media presence—we've established the four pillars of your author brand. These are crucial components that should be in every author's branding toolkit, laying the groundwork upon which you can build further. If you don't do anything else, these are the four essential parts of your brand that you should put in place.

While these four essentials set you on the right path, there are other steps you can take to expand your brand and give it that extra spark. It's all about showcasing the unique author that you are and ensuring your brand is not just visible, but unforgettable. From author blogs and book trailers to professional photos and consistent branding, these are not just extras but significant boosters to increase your author brand's reach and impact. They're your chance to share more of you with your readers, and trust me, they're going to love it.

So, how can you add that extra sparkle to your brand and make waves in the world of publishing? Here are some additional steps that will make your brand shine.

1. Author Blog:

Maintaining an author blog can be a powerful tool to engage with your readers and build a loyal community around your brand. You can share behind-the-scenes content, insights about your writing process, or any topic that aligns with your books or genre. Remember, consistency is key – regular updates can help keep your readers engaged and eager for more.

Exercise: Brainstorm a list of potential blog post topics. Aim for a balance of promotional content (like book teasers or release dates) and value-added content (like writing tips or genre-related discussions).

2. Book Trailer:

A professional, engaging book trailer can generate buzz and anticipation for your upcoming releases. It serves as a visual elevator pitch for your book and can be shared across your website, social media, and Amazon Author Central account.

Exercise: Sketch out a storyboard for your book trailer. What key scenes or themes do you want to highlight? Remember, it should capture the essence of your book without giving too much away.

3. Professional Author Photos:

High-quality, professional author photos contribute significantly to your brand's image. They can be used across all platforms - your website, social media, book covers, and even promotional materials. These photos should match the tone and style of your brand.

Exercise: Plan your author's photo shoot. What kind of setting, outfits, and poses best express your brand?

4. Book Reviews:

Book reviews are vital to influencing potential readers and boosting your book's visibility. Develop a strategy to garner reviews, such as reaching out to book bloggers, offering Advanced Reader Copies (ARCs), or encouraging readers through your newsletter and social media platforms.

Exercise: Draft a polite and friendly email asking for a book review. Be sure to express your gratitude for their time and consider offering a free copy of your book.

5. Consistent Author Branding:

Maintaining a consistent visual brand across all platforms is vital. This includes your logo (if you have one), colour palette, typography, and imagery style. Consistency helps create brand recognition and resonates with your target audience.

Exercise: Create a style guide for your brand that includes your chosen colour palette, typography, and imagery style.

6. Networking:

Engaging with online communities and forums related to your genre can help you establish relationships with potential readers and other authors. It's an opportunity to learn, share insights, and even collaborate. Remember, genuine engagement is more valuable than promotional posts.

Exercise: Identify three online communities or forums where your target readers might be present. Participate in conversations and aim to contribute valuable insights rather than overtly promote your book.

7. Book Listings:

Ensure your books are listed on all major online bookstores and platforms, like Goodreads. These platforms are where your readers are looking for their next read. Keeping your listings updated with your latest releases, accurate descriptions, and engaging cover images is crucial.

Exercise: Check your book listings on different platforms. Ensure the descriptions are accurate, the cover images are high resolution, and all the information is up-to-date.

8. Guest Blogging/Podcast Interviews:

Guest blogging or appearing on podcast interviews can be an effective way to increase your visibility and reach. It helps position you as an expert in your field, provides value to the host's audience, and brings your books to the attention of new readers.

Exercise: Identify three blogs or podcasts that align with your genre or writing style. Consider how you can provide value to their audience – could you offer insights into your writing process, share tips for other writers, or discuss the themes in your books?

And there you have it: the four essential steps to building a robust author brand and eight additional extras that will elevate your brand even further. While this may seem like a hefty list, remember that building a brand doesn't happen overnight. It's a gradual process that involves consistent efforts and a deep understanding of who you are as an author and who your readers are.

Always keep in mind that the core of your author brand is the unique voice and value you bring to your readers. Every decision you make, from the design of your website to the tone of your social media posts, should reflect this. Stay true to yourself and your vision, and let your passion shine through every aspect of your brand.

Before I finish this chapter I think it's important to remind you of one thing: "Done is better than perfect." Building your author brand isn't about flawlessly executing each of these steps from day one. Rather, it's about making a start, however imperfect it may be.

Not every step might apply to your unique situation, and that's perfectly okay. The real key is to start somewhere. Pick a few steps that resonate with you the most and begin there. As you move forward, you'll learn what works best for you and your brand.

Remember, every successful author's journey began with that first imperfect step. It's okay if you don't have all the answers right now or if everything doesn't fall perfectly into place. What's important is that you're taking action, learning, and evolving along the way.

Finally, remember to evaluate your brand regularly. As you grow as an author and as your readership expands, your brand might need to evolve. Stay flexible and open to changes, and keep your readers at the heart of every decision you make.

This is your journey, and you have the power to shape it in the way that best suits you and your dreams. Building a strong author brand might be challenging, but the rewards are enormous. So, take these twelve steps, make them your own, and start building the author brand you've always dreamed of. You've got this!

Chapter Ten

Expanding Your Brand

Selling Digital Products

It's time to diversify your income streams!

You've already honed your skills in creating engaging and visually appealing content as a writer and creator of low-content books. Now, it's time to think about how you can expand your publishing brand by diversifying your revenue streams. One way to do this is by creating and selling digital products. By writing and creating low-content books, you have developed and acquired a set of specific skills that are easily transferable to other products that you can sell besides your books. These skills include design, layout, and formatting, as well as the ability to create visually appealing and user-friendly content. It's amazing to think about all the different opportunities that you can explore with the skills you've acquired! One area where these skills can be applied is in the creation of digital products.

Digital products are a great way to reach a larger audience and have a wider impact. They can be created quickly, easily, and at a low cost, and they can be sold over and over again. Here are some examples of digital products that you can create and sell to expand your publishing brand:

eBooks: eBooks are a popular digital product that can be sold on platforms such as Amazon Kindle Direct Publishing or Barnes & Noble Press. As a writer, you have the ability to create engaging and well-written content that can be used in eBooks. Additionally, your skills in layout and formatting can be used to create visually appealing eBooks that are easy to read and navigate.

One of the main advantages of eBooks is their accessibility. They can be easily downloaded and read on a variety of devices, such as the Kindle, iPad, or smartphones. This means that you have the potential to reach a wider audience with your eBooks than you would with physical books.

Another advantage of eBooks is that they can be easily updated and republished. This means that if you make changes or find errors in your eBook, you can quickly fix them and republish the updated version. This is not possible with physical books, which can be costly and time-consuming to update.

When creating an eBook, it's important to consider the format and layout. Ebooks can be in a variety of formats, such as Kindle, PDF, or ePub. Each format has its own set of requirements and limitations, so it's important to research the best format for your eBook. Additionally, the layout and formatting of your eBook should be visually appealing and easy to read. This can include using headings, subheadings, bullet points, and images to break up the text and make it more readable.

Promoting your eBook is also an essential step in the process. You can use social media, email marketing, and other online platforms to promote your eBook. Additionally, you can reach out to book bloggers and reviewers to get your eBook reviewed and gain more visibility.

In a nutshell, eBooks can be a fantastic avenue for growing your publishing brand and connecting with a larger audience. You've got the skills, the creativity, and the drive to create amazing digital products. With the right approach, eBooks can open up a whole new world of opportunities, helping you diversify your income and reach for the stars!

Online courses: Are you ready to turn up the heat and amplify your reach? With your rich experience in writing and low-content book creation, you're sitting on a goldmine of wisdom that can be shared with the world. The stage is set for you to create your very own online courses!

Online courses can be a powerful way to share your unique insights and expertise. Picture this: students from every corner of the globe learning from your experiences and techniques at their own pace, in the comfort of their homes. Not only do these courses allow you to impact lives far and wide, but they're also an excellent way to turn your know-how into a steady stream of passive income.

Designing an online course can be an adventure in itself! Consider whether you'd like to create a self-paced course, offering learners the freedom to soak up your content whenever they please. Or perhaps you would prefer a live, interactive course with scheduled classes that allow real-time interaction and engagement.

The format of your course content is another key decision. Would your knowledge be best conveyed via video lessons, audio files, or written materials? Perhaps a mix of all three?

When it comes to course length, there's no one-size-fits-all. Whether you go for a compact course with a few intense modules or a longer, more leisurely-paced one spread over weeks, the choice depends on your subject matter, the depth of expertise you're sharing, and the time you need to comprehensively cover the topic.

Of course, even the best course needs a spotlight to shine. Promoting your course is where your creativity can really shine! Using social media, your email marketing know-how, and other online platforms can help you spread the word about your course. Reach out to influencers, bloggers, and other mavens in your field for potential collaborations—it's all about getting the word out there!

In a nutshell, crafting an online course is an incredibly rewarding way to share your unique wisdom with the world and monetize your skills simultaneously. Whether it's the format, structure, length, or promotion strategy, each aspect of your course has the power to make it shine. With the right approach, an online course can not only enhance your publishing brand but also offer an exciting new way to diversify your revenue streams. So, are you ready to embark on this exciting new journey? The world of online courses is waiting for you to make your mark!

Printables: If you're not familiar, printables are delightful digital treasures that customers can download and print out for countless uses. Whether it's sprucing up their planner, decking their walls, or bringing some fun to a party with custom games, printables have got it covered! As a talented writer or low-content book creator, you're perfectly equipped to whip up appealing, high-quality printables.

The beauty of printables is their adaptability. Think of them as chameleons; they can fit into a myriad of situations, either personal or commercial. Imagine designing planner inserts, to-do lists, or budget sheets that make someone's daily routine more manageable. Or perhaps creating stunning wall art, enticing signs, or eye-catching invitations for commercial use. The versatility of printables means your audience can be as diverse as your designs.

An added bonus? Printables are masters of customization! You can offer a template that your customers can jazz up with their own text, images, or other elements, creating a unique product that speaks directly to their needs and style.

But let's not forget design and layout—it's where your creativity gets to shine! Aim to create printables that are not only eye-catching but also easy to understand and use. Use visual techniques like headings, bullet points, and images to make the content digestible and engaging. And remember, the size, resolution, and file format of your printable also matter!

Of course, your amazing printables need a little spotlight! Promoting them effectively is key. You've got this! Leverage social media, your email marketing prowess, and other online platforms to strut your printables' stuff. Teaming up with bloggers, influencers, and other experts in your field for collaborations can also give your printables the push they deserve.

Did I mention one of my brands thrives on selling printables that complement my low-content books? They've found a loving home on Etsy and my brand's website. Who knows, your printables might be the next big hit!

With their wide-ranging appeal, customization options, and your own creative skillset, you're all set to create stellar printables that captivate your audience. Remember, it's not just about creating them but also promoting them effectively. By adding printables to your arsenal, you're not just expanding your publishing brand; you're embracing an engaging way to diversify your income streams.

Webinars: Have you ever thought about sharing your knowledge in real-time? Enter the world of webinars! As a writer, you're a pro at crafting engaging, educational content. Couple that with your public speaking and communication skills, and voila! You're a webinar wizard in the making!

Webinars are a beautiful blend of information sharing and interactivity. They offer this superpower of chatting with your attendees live, answering queries on the spot, and addressing concerns. It's like hosting a cosy little gathering right in your digital living room, creating a sense of community and connection that eBooks or pre-recorded videos might not fully replicate.

Guess what else? Webinars are sneaky little lead generators! They offer a platform to introduce your products or services and build a healthy lead database. Fancy offering an exclusive deal or promotion that's only for your webinar attendees? It's a proven recipe to increase conversions and sales figures.

When it comes to designing your webinar, let's think about the format and structure. Will it be a lively Q&A session, a thoughtful panel discussion, or maybe a solo presentation where you captivate the audience with your expertise? And don't forget the logistics—the length of the webinar and the date and time that would best suit your lovely audience.

As for promoting your webinar, your best bet is to rally your social media platforms, ace your email marketing game, and harness other online avenues. Don't shy away from reaching out to influencers, bloggers, or experts in your field for potential collaborations—the more, the merrier!

Webinars are your ticket to a live, engaging platform where you can dish out your knowledge and expertise. They not only diversify your revenue streams and boost your publishing brand, but they can also reel in leads and rev up your conversion rate.

Templates: Let's chat about something that can make our lives a whole lot easier—templates. These are like your creative wingman—a pre-designed layout you can easily adapt for your own needs. Think of them as a jumping-off point or a blueprint to make your work shine professionally and consistently. And as a writer and low-content book creator, you're well-equipped to whip up templates that are as gorgeous as they are functional.

Templates are like the Swiss Army knife of content creation. They can be tailored for a whole bunch of projects, whether personal or commercial. You could be crafting templates for low-content books, eBooks, planners, and resumes—the sky's the limit! This versatility makes them a firm favourite among a diverse group of customers and audiences.

Now, as a fiction or non-fiction author, you can put on your creative cap and develop a bunch of templates to streamline your writing process, spice up your marketing game, or offer them as appealing lead magnets or products. Let me toss some ideas your way:

1. Plot Outline Templates: These can guide fiction authors to weave together a compelling plot, sculpt character arcs, and shape scenes.

2. Character Profile Templates: These buddies help authors mould their characters in depth, organising everything from physical traits to their unique backstory.

3. World-building Templates: Perfect for our fantasy and sci-fi authors out there, these help you draft immersive settings brimming with geographical, cultural, political, and historical details.

4. Writing Schedule Templates: Every author, fiction or non-fiction, can stay organised with a plan to manage their writing time, set deadlines, and track their progress.

5. Chapter Outline Templates: Nonfiction authors can map out their chapters, helping them organise their main ideas, supporting points, research notes, and sources.

6. Marketing and Promotion Templates: Design press releases, social media posts, email campaigns, or event planning templates to turbocharge your marketing efforts.

7. Book Signing or Event Planning Templates: To plan book signings, workshops, or other events, covering everything from venue, budget, marketing materials, and guest lists.

By crafting templates that meet your needs and those of your fellow authors, you can boost your writing process, save some time, and offer valuable resources to your peers.

Templates are a game-changer when it comes to saving time and effort. Why start from scratch when you can simply fill in the blanks? They give you a head start, freeing you from fretting over design details.

But remember, when you're making templates, the design and layout matter. Your templates should be easy on the eyes and easy to use, so don't forget to use headings, subheadings, bullet points, and images, and think about the template format—Word document, PDF, or otherwise.

And once your templates are ready for the world, it's time to promote them! You can work your magic on social media, ace your email marketing, and use other online platforms. Feel free to collaborate with bloggers, influencers, or experts in your field; teamwork makes the dream work!

So, templates? They're an excellent tool to assist others with their projects and grow your publishing brand. As a writer and low-content book creator, you're in a prime position to craft visually stunning, user-friendly templates. Keep in mind the design, layout, format, and promotion strategies when creating them. Done right, templates can be a jewel in your publishing crown and help diversify your income. They are a time-saving, polish-adding resource for the user, and honestly, a creator's best friend!

Virtual Assistance: Have you ever thought of becoming a virtual assistant? It's a fantastic way to use your writing or low-content book creation skills to help others. You could be the go-to person for other writers, authors, or entrepreneurs who need help with tasks like editing, formatting, or research.

What's amazing about being a virtual assistant? Well, for starters, it's all about flexibility. You can work from your couch, a coffee shop, or a beach in Bali—anywhere with an internet connection, really! Plus, you get to set your own schedule, working around other commitments or even your favourite TV show's airtime.

Another big plus of being a virtual assistant is the steady income. Once you establish your reputation, you can juggle tasks for multiple clients, which can mean a nice regular paycheck coming in.

But before you dive in, remember a few key things. Firstly, make sure you're clear about what services you offer. Don't leave any room for misunderstandings; lay out the scope of your work, the timeline, and your rates upfront. And remember, communication is key. Whether it's by email, phone, or video call, stay in touch with your clients to keep things running smoothly.

Let's not forget about promoting your services. You're not going to get clients if they don't know you exist, right? Use social media, email marketing, or other online platforms to spread the word about what you do. Reach out to other writers, authors, or entrepreneurs directly; offer them your services and let them see how you can help them.

To sum it up, virtual assistance is a fantastic way to put your skills to work, help others, and bring in some cash. You'll enjoy the freedom of setting your own schedule and the opportunity to work with diverse clients. Just remember that clarity about your services, good communication, and a bit of self-promotion are essential. With all these ingredients, you can take your publishing brand to the next level. Who knows, being a virtual assistant might just be the next big thing in your career!

Let's talk about printables

Of all the products mentioned, my personal favourites are the printables. They're not only super easy and accessible for us writers or low-content book creators, but also a lot of fun to make. Best part? You don't need to be a tech whiz or a design pro to get started. With handy tools like Canva, Illustrator, or even good ol' Microsoft Word, anyone can hop on the printable train.

Crafting printables is a wonderful way to let your creative juices flow. Use your knack for design to create products that are not only easy on the eyes but also user-friendly. And don't forget your mighty pen (or keyboard, in this case)! Use your writing prowess to whip up engaging content like instructions or patterns to include in your printable. It's like wearing two hats—the writer and the designer—at the same time!

One of the best things about printables is that they're not time- or resource-hogs. Once you've got a template in place, you can easily tweak it to churn out multiple versions of the same product. It's like having a creative conveyor belt—no need to start from scratch each time.

And guess what? Printables are like chameleons; they can adapt to a myriad of uses, both personal and commercial. This makes them a hit with a wide array of customers. You can create anything from planner inserts, wall art, and décor to entertaining games. Plus, you can tailor them to suit various occasions like weddings, birthdays, or holidays.

In short, printables are a simple and accessible path for writers or low-content book creators like us. They're a fantastic way to express your creativity, showcase your writing and design skills, and make good use of your time and resources. With printables, expanding your publishing brand and reaching a broader audience is a breeze. Plus, they offer a brilliant way to add some variety to your revenue streams while allowing you to explore your passion for design. So, why not give it a shot?

Where can you sell your printables, or other digital products for that matter?

If you're looking to sell your printables, let me introduce you to one of my favourite platforms: Etsy. It's like a bustling online bazaar brimming with people hungry for unique, handcrafted items. In other words, it's the perfect place to showcase your amazing printables!

What makes Etsy so great, you ask? Well, for starters, it's got a massive, active community of eager buyers. This means there are heaps of potential customers already browsing the site, just waiting to discover your creative printables. Plus, with Etsy's super handy search feature, it's a breeze for these folks to find and fall in love with your products.

Setting up shop on Etsy is a piece of cake. Within a few minutes, you can create an account, sprinkle some magic on your virtual storefront, and start listing your products. What's more, Etsy comes packed with all sorts of bells and whistles to help you run your shop smoothly and promote your products, from detailed analytics to targeted advertising options.

Did you know that Etsy can even help grow your online presence beyond the platform? You're allowed to include a link to your own website in your shop profile and product listings. This means that your customers can learn more about you, check out your other offerings, and even sign up for your newsletter or follow you on social media. Just remember to keep an eye on Etsy's rules, as they may change over time.

So, to wrap things up, Etsy is a wonderful marketplace to sell your printables. It offers a ready audience craving your unique, creative products and a plethora of tools to help you manage and promote your shop. Plus, it provides an opportunity to draw Etsy visitors to your own website, boosting your brand's visibility. With Etsy, expanding your publishing brand and reaching more people is a cinch!

What kind of printables can publishers sell on Etsy that relate to their books?

Fiction, non-fiction, and low content Book writers can create a variety of printables to complement their books, engage with their audience, or offer as lead magnets. Some examples include:

1. **Fiction authors:**

- Reading group discussion guides with questions and conversation starters

- Character profiles or illustrations

- Maps and timelines of the story's setting

- Printable bookmarks with quotes from the book

- Colouring pages inspired by the story or characters

1. **Non-fiction authors:**

- Worksheets or workbooks to help readers apply the concepts from the book

- Checklists, summaries, or quick reference guides related to the book's topic

- Inspirational quotes or affirmations from the book as posters or wall art

- Templates or planners to help readers organise their thoughts and ideas

- Infographics or visual aids that explain complex concepts

1. **Low-content book creators:**

- Colouring pages with intricate designs or patterns

- Journal or planner pages with various layouts and prompts

- Crossword puzzles, word searches, or Sudoku puzzles

- Habit trackers or goal-setting worksheets

- Calendars, daily planners, or weekly planners with unique designs

These are just a few examples of the types of printables that authors can sell on Etsy that relate to their books. When brainstorming printable ideas, the magic word is "relevance". Think about what your readers might find handy, intriguing, or downright delightful to complement their reading experience. Maybe a character development worksheet for your latest fantasy novel? Or how about a chic planner that reflects the tone of your self-help guide? Let your imagination run wild!

So you're ready to start selling on Etsy? Awesome! Here are some golden nuggets to keep in mind:

Firstly, let's talk about finding your niche. Think about your low-content books or your writing genre and who your target audience is. By choosing a niche that's in line with your creations, you're sure to catch the eye of your ideal customers.

Next up: quality. Nobody can resist a good-looking, high-quality printable. So ensure your printables are visually attractive and top-notch. It'll not only make your brand shine, but also leave your customers smiling.

Then there's your Etsy listing. Use relevant keywords, write clear descriptions, and upload high-quality images to make your products pop. Adding appropriate tags will also make it easier for customers to find your amazing printables.

Don't forget to spread the word! Social media, email marketing, or even partnering with fellow creators can be effective ways to promote your printables and attract more customers.

Customer service is crucial. Be prompt and kind when handling customer inquiries and concerns. It's a surefire way to build a loyal customer base.

Use Etsy's analytics to understand your sales and your customers better.

Finally, keep the ball rolling. Consistently creating and listing new printables will keep your shop fresh and appealing to new customers.

In a nutshell, selling printables on Etsy offers a fantastic opportunity for you to reach new readers and grow your revenue. By carving out the right niche, creating dazzling printables, optimising your listings, and being customer-friendly, you'll be well on your way to becoming a go-to name in your niche. And remember, the ultimate goal is to guide these Etsy shoppers right back to your own website, where they can discover your fantastic books!

"Discover new horizons for your author brand by venturing into the realm of digital products, where the only limit is your imagination."

Chapter Eleven

You Did It!

A Closing Note

And just like that, you've turned the final page! Give yourself a pat on the back—you've made it through, and you're now ready to super-charge your publishing business. I truly hope you find joy and value in reading this book, just as I did in writing it. We've travelled quite a bit together, and I couldn't be more proud of you for staying the course.

I'd like to take a moment to appreciate the game-changer that is branding for us, authors. Throughout our exploration, we've delved into the magic of branding, highlighting how it can foster a deep connection with your audience, let your unique voice echo, and turbocharge your book sales. My sincere wish is that these nuggets of wisdom inspire and support you as you chart your own unique journey in the vibrant world of self-publishing.

In the chapters we've traversed together, we've unveiled different facets of author branding, right from shaping an enticing author website to leveraging the might of social media and nurturing a dedicated email list. But remember, this is just the tip of the iceberg! There's a wealth of strategies and tools out there waiting to reinforce your brand and widen your audience. As you stride forward, keep nurturing your curiosity, daring to experiment, and constantly evolving your strategies to stay in sync with your audience.

It's vital to remember that your brand is a reflection of you—your beliefs and your distinct voice as a writer. Embrace your uniqueness and let your authentic voice echo in everything you create. By doing this, you'll not only attract readers who resonate with your narrative, but you'll also find a sense of fulfilment and purpose in your work. Branding isn't a one-and-done deal; it's a continuous journey. Keep exploring, keep absorbing new knowledge, and most importantly, don't fear those missteps. Your brand, much like life itself, is an ever-evolving entity, and as your business blooms, your brand will flourish along with it. So stay open-minded and never stop experimenting.

Before we part, here's a gentle reminder: be patient with yourself. Building a robust author brand is a marathon, not a sprint. If you occasionally feel swamped or uncertain, that's perfectly okay! The key is to persevere, take baby steps, and celebrate every win, however small. Believe in your abilities and your passion for writing and creating, and know that you have something truly unique and valuable to offer the world.

A huge thank you for embarking on this journey with me. I hope this book serves as a faithful guide in your quest to build a prosperous publishing business. Stay in touch, and do share your progress—I'm rooting for you every step of the way.

Until we cross paths again, keep those creative juices flowing and continue expanding your brand!

Chapter Twelve

What Next?

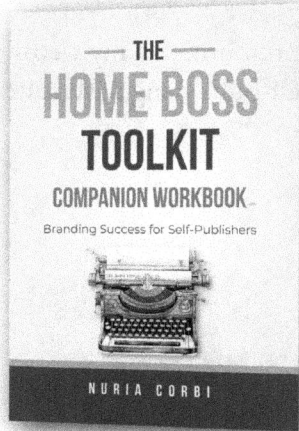

Once you've immersed yourself in the strategies and insights of "The Home Boss Toolkit: Mastering Branding for Self-Publishers," you might be wondering, "What's next? How do I put all this valuable knowledge into action?

That's where "The Home Boss Toolkit Companion Workbook" comes in! Designed as the perfect companion to your main guide, this workbook takes the theories and strategies from "The Home Boss Toolkit" and turns them into practical, actionable steps tailored to your unique author brand.

In this hands-on workbook, you'll find a variety of engaging activities, structured exercises, and thought-provoking questions, all designed to help you implement the knowledge you've gained and create your own personalised marketing plan. Plus, the bonus pages at the end are perfect for brainstorming, doodling, and dreaming big.

Whether you're new to marketing or a seasoned pro, this workbook will help you further develop your skills, boost your confidence, and turn your self-publishing dreams into reality.

So, why wait? Grab your favourite pen and "The Home Boss Toolkit Workbook," and let's dive deeper into the exciting world of branding for self-publishers. Your journey to marketing success continues here!

Scan the code for more resources on my website to help you on your self-publishing adventure